Personal Development Made Simple

Better Health, Fitness, Finances and Relationships

Robert J DeVito

DEDICATION

My life has been one of great fortune. I have been in the right place at the right time more than anyone I know. My luckiest moment was paying attention when Nicole walked into my life. With you, my life is complete. Together our family (Robert, Nicole, Nicholas, Anthony and Macy) brings me the ultimate joy and success. I love you.

CONTENTS

ACKNOWLEDGMENTS

My personal definition of success is maintaining life balance. I measure my success daily by how often I can coax a smile from others, and how often others make me laugh. There are many people who seem to know how to amuse me often. Through the gift of technology, Eric, Jeff, Kevin and Nicole make me laugh multiple times a day.

Another measurement of success to me is the ability to think clearly, to innovate and produce results. Jay and Bryan from Dynamic Health and Fitness embody Human Performance and Leadership. I am proud to call them business partners and even prouder to call them friends.

Lastly, to me success is measured in commitment and consistency. The clients of Innovation Fitness Solutions and My Dynamic Life inspire me on a daily basis to continue striving for excellence and to maintain my work ethic by serving them.

To all, I thank you.

INTRODUCTION

Personal Development can have many layers. The process of continued growth should never stop. I believe that 'Simple' will allow you to experience growth quickly and accurately. This book is short and concise. To me, success is personal and cannot be defined for you. You must do that for yourself. Coincidentally, I believe defining success for you **IS** a key to success.

Wiktionary defines success as:
success (*plural* successes**)**
The achievement of one's aim or goal.
His third attempt to pass the entrance exam was a success.
(*Business*) financial profitability.
One who, or that which, achieves assumed goals.
Scholastically, he was a success.
The new range of toys has been a resounding success.

A few of the synonyms that stick out: achievement and accomplishment. These are important words to me. I believe we all desire to be successful in our lives. I have not known many people that set out to be mediocre or less. So, this book is for the achievers. The chances are quite good that you are incredibly successful in areas of your life, yet struggle in other areas. An example would be that you are a wonderful, caring parent but have not seen the career success that you feel you deserve or that you are capable of. *Personal Development Made Simple* will simply get you to become aware of what works for you, how it works, and why it works. It will also make you aware of your hurting habits and how you have been stalling yourself in other areas. If you consistently apply these proven strategies in the other areas of life, you will succeed.

When I began to compile this book the concept itself came from Napoleon Hill's classic work *Think! And Grow Rich*. In it he interviews 100's of the world's most successful people and finds the commonality in their stories, actions, and outcomes. This book will simplify the topic of achieving success.

In my work I see people at different stages of the success spectrum. I have an opportunity on a daily basis to see people that are just starting their new journey, I see others that are "In Process", yet I see others that anyone evaluating them would deem to be highly successful and still they continue to strive for more.

A commonality I see in each and every one of these courageous people is that their overall goals can be described as a search for happiness, peace and fulfillment.

With that in mind, I present *Personal Development Made Simple* as a guidebook for successful long-term achievement. The concepts and strategies within are designed to aid you in achieving and <u>maintaining</u> happiness and fulfillment.

These concepts and strategies can be applied to any area of life. I commonly use them for Health, Fitness, Family and Finance purposes. They flow seamlessly from one to the next. When you consistently apply proven principles (C.A.P.P) progress will come.

There are three basic sections of this book:

What makes up a successful person? How do they think and what makes them tick? Starting from their thought process and character through their decision making and actions.

The second section depicts the habits and essential components in life of highly successful people. We do things differently, don't we?

Lastly, I deliver the Tools to Plan for, act on, review and manage success in all of life's arenas.

In the worst case, this book will simplify things for you.

In the best case, it will serve as a guide to a more productive and fulfilling life.

My long held belief is that we must take a WHOLEistic approach to our success to truly appreciate and enjoy life's pleasures. We will discuss habits and ideas to best care for you in mind and body. Success takes energy. Having energy means taking care of you. Focus on remaining positive, planning for success, and preparing for setbacks. If we can do these 3 simple, yet, vital things, we will achieve...

To your success,

Robert J DeVito

OVERVIEW

This page is an updated version of the Philosophy found in *90 Days to a New You*. *'90 Days'* was my first published book. The philosophy remains true and solid. I have updated it to fit the message of this book. Own these concepts. Chapter 1 begins to delve into the specific actions needed to achieve from these concepts.

The first lesson is - **CONSISTENCY**. Consistency is achieved by following *Realistic, Progressive and Maintainable* strategies for long-term results. This is the cornerstone of continued development and success. Doing something once or for a short period of time is *Consistent Inconsistency* and will lead us in a circle of stops and starts. Choose to perform and continue that performance.

The next lesson is - *You* **CONTROL** *your environment - your environment does not have control over you.*

In life, you are free to choose what you do or do not do. The decisions and choices that you make; the habits that you form determine your outcome. That means that you are in control, and you are responsible for your actions. This is both powerful and empowering.

Finally, the third lesson is -**PLAN.** You have to be aware of your surroundings and make a plan that is realistic for you. Any good plan has a direct route and an infinite number of alternate routes. We all know that perfection does not exist, so stop trying to attain and execute the perfect plan. You ultimately will fail. For long-term success, I recommend that you think in terms of "better bad" or "progress; not perfection". Look for ways to enjoy life's little pleasures but be accountable for your actions. Look for ways to move more during the day, not only in the gym but at the office and at home as well. Most importantly, <u>stay positive</u>. Remember that one meal does not "blow it" and missing one workout does not destroy your week or one missed opportunity does not make it impossible to achieve the goal that you chose. The only way you will not succeed long-term is by giving up.

Inaction breeds failure. Action breeds achievement.

We are what we repeatedly do. Excellence, then, is not an act but a habit. –Aristotle

Control

Consistency

Planning

Stay Positive -- Plan Ahead -- Rebound from Setbacks

EVERYTHING AFFECTS EVERYTHING

To work toward wellness, it's important to focus on six different components of life, including:

Emotional Wellness - People who are emotionally well are able to express their feelings freely. They know how to handle the stress of their daily lives and know when and how to seek support from others. They also work to develop healthy relationships with others.

Intellectual Wellness - Ongoing education is important for intellectual wellness. People who are intellectually well enjoy learning new things, expressing their creativity, and improving their skills. An example of this is the fact that you are reading this book.

Physical Wellness - Proper nutrition, exercise and other healthy habits are all part of physical wellness. People who are working on their physical wellness avoid the use of tobacco, drugs and excessive alcohol. They also seek proper medical care when necessary—including getting preventative testing.

Social Wellness - People with social wellness contribute to their community by maintaining healthy relationships with a variety of people—despite any differences in background or ethnic origin. They practice good communication skills with everyone they meet and when conflict arises, they work to resolve it in a healthy manner.

Spiritual Wellness - People who are spiritually well spend time thinking about their own beliefs and values and strive to find a source of inner peace and strength. This "soul searching" may involve a relationship with a "higher power" which helps them deal with the ongoing challenges that life brings.

Professional Wellness - People that are happy in their jobs are happier overall, are more productive. less stressed and generally take action on their ideas.

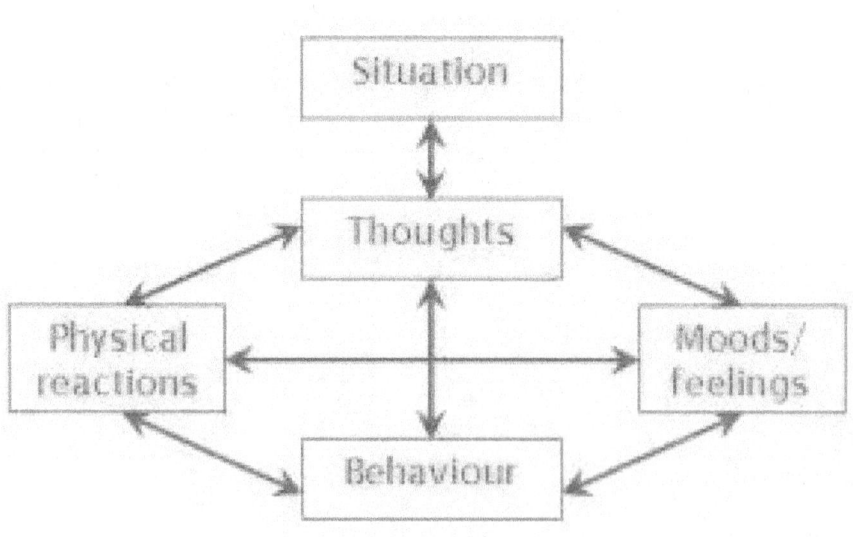

CHAPTER 1

SUCCESSFUL PEOPLE

Chapter 1 will dive into the character traits, habits and mindset of high performing individuals. This sets up the model for success to follow.

We do not need to create a magic formula. It has been created thousands of times before. We simply need to be aware of it and apply the principles to our own lives.

While reading these chapters make notes on the habits and traits that you already possess. Congratulate yourself for being so awesome AND evaluate the habits and traits that you need to minimize or add to your life to improve your success.

 Habits + Time = Results

Habits: helping us or hurting us? Habits will determine your energy levels, your health, and your life's performance. Are your habits getting you want you want?

HABITS DETERMINE OUTCOMES

Why have you been so successful in reaching some of your goals, but not others? If you aren't sure, you are far from alone in your confusion. It turns out that even brilliant, highly accomplished people are pretty lousy when it comes to understanding why they succeed or fail. The intuitive answer — that you are born predisposed to certain talents and lacking in others — is really just one small piece of the puzzle. In fact, decades of research on achievement suggests that successful people reach their goals not simply because of who they are, but more often because of what they do.

High Performance Living. This is what I call success. It is about having energy needed to thrive and persevere on a daily basis. It is about having the insight to see the obstacles and avoid them or the endurance to withstand them. Performance living is about living life to its fullest. The only way to truly accomplish this is by having the energy, vitality, resilience, and physical well-being which allows for it. Performance living is all about the habits we live by on a daily basis. I have seen people with unimaginable hindrances live the best life possible in spite of their restrictions, but I have also met many with more muscle and hustle lead the most low-performance lifestyle possible. So much of the quality of our lives is dependent on our habits. Most of our behaviors are unconscious and automatic - they are learned, and so, they too can be **UN**learned. If the desire is strong enough for long enough, you can create different and better habits to create a High Performance Lifestyle.

Your habits determine your outcomes. Your goals are all dependent on your mindset, nutrition, movement, and recovery and planning. They require conscious positive choices that create healthy and productive habits that set the stage for excellence. Most of all, your goals require a commitment to taking care of the most important thing ever…YOU!!! Your results are dependent upon your actions and your actions are a result of your thoughts, feelings, behaviors and actions.

Take the time to get to know yourself before saying "I want to lose 10lbs." Get yourself a journal and figure out on a scale of 1-10 (10 being highest) what your performance life is at this point. Identify the habits that have helped you in life thus far, and the ones that have hurt you along the way. Be honest with yourself in writing and look at it every day. Write it down as it comes along and learn from it. I guarantee you will be better tomorrow because of it.

KEYS TO HIGH-PERFORMANCE LIVING

For you to be at the top of your form, to be action oriented, fast moving, and extremely productive, you have to have high levels of physical and mental energy.

For you to be able to take advantage of all the opportunities around you, and to have the continuous enthusiasm that keeps you and others motivated and moving ahead, you have to organize your life so that you feel great about yourself most of the time. You will need to work hard…and play hard, too!

Successful people get up early, they rarely complain, they expect performance from others ,and they expect extraordinary performance from themselves. Repeated, high-level success starts with a recognition that hard work pays off.

Personal Development is all about working on ourselves and never quitting. Successful people work on their personality, their leadership skills, management skills, relationships and every other detail of life.

So, here are the essential keys for repeated, long-term success.

1. Feed your Body the Right Foods. The first key to high energy is the proper feeding of your body and mind. To perform at your best, you must eat the right foods, in the right balance, and in the right combination. Your diet has an inordinate impact on the amount of energy you have, how well you sleep, your levels of health and fitness, your mood, decision making and your performance throughout the day and into the evening.

Fueling your body means eating a clean, healthy diet and is another way of sending the message to yourself that you value yourself enough to feed your body only the best. Avoid processed foods. Focus on foods that are fresh, like vegetables and fruits, whole grains, and lean proteins. Remember to avoid the salt and sugar. A healthy diet keeps your hormones in balance, and makes for a healthier, happier, more confident YOU!

2. Watch your Weight. The second key to high energy is proper weight. Proper weight is essential for health, happiness, and long life. If you are not happy with your current level of physical health, you need to set specific goals for yourself for the weeks and months ahead. High-Performance Living would suggest that you keep tabs on your weight weekly.

3. Exercise is Essential. The third key to high energy is exercise. Exercise raises your serotonin levels (the "happy" hormones). It gives you confidence when you overcome physical challenges. It also gives you a sense of accomplishment and it's a way of telling yourself, "I value you." Exercising sends you a message that you are worth taking the time out for yourself to make your body and mind healthier and stronger.

The best activity for high energy and high levels of fitness is cross-training. This type of exercise is fast paced; circuit style training that gets your heart rate high. It strengthens the body while improving cardiovascular fitness. This type of training is not for beginners, so be sure to start with a progressive plan.

4. (3R) - Get Lots of Rest and Recreation and Recovery. The fourth key to high energy is proper rest. You need an average of seven to eight hours of sleep each night to be fully rested. You need to take off at least one full day each week during which you don't work at all. You should take regular mini-holidays of two or three days each, every couple of months. You should take one and two week vacations each year when you relax completely and get your mind totally off your work.

5. Develop a Positive Mental Attitude. The fifth key to high energy is the reduction or elimination of negative emotions. This can be the most important thing you do to assure a long and happy life. Your ability to keep your mind on what you want, and off of what you don't want, will determine your levels of health and happiness more than any other decision you make. Live in the solution, not in the issue. Go on a positive mental attitude diet, one day at a time. Resolve that, for the today, you are going to keep your mind on what you want and keep it off the things you don't want. You are going to think and talk positively and optimistically about your goals, other people, and everything that is going on in your life.

Eliminate "can't" and "but" from your vocabulary. Those obstacles that can get in your way when working toward a goal, typically come from a lot of self statements that begin with "can't" and "but." Take a day to just catch yourself, and note how many times you use those two self defeating words. The next day, turn those two words into "can," and completely eliminate "but" from your vocabulary. No excuses... you CAN do anything you truly set your mind to! As you accomplish those goals that you CAN accomplish, your self esteem will sky rocket.

6. Start a Personal Mental Fitness Program. The sixth key to high energy is for you to increase your Mental Fitness. If you are a television watcher, then, control how much "fluff" you watch and add in high quality/educational programming. Be sure to add 20 minutes of reading to your Mental Diet daily.

7. Become a Powerhouse. The more you practice the health habits we have talked about, the more energy and vitality you will have. The more you keep your conversation focused on your goals and on the things you want, the greater the amount of strength and power you will feel. You will be more alert and aware. You will feel more positive and action oriented in every situation.

8. Get quality sleep. As you've heard it said many times before, it is important for an adult to get quality sleep between 7-9 hours a night. Structure your day so that you will be able to wind down prior to your bedtime and have that quality sleep your body needs and deserves. The earlier you have to get up, the earlier you need to go to bed. It's a great way to rest from the stress of the previous day, and re-energize for the upcoming day.

9. Surround yourself with people that encourage you. As typical human beings we tend to be very hard on ourselves. We are our toughest critics. The last thing we need to is spend time with people that are critical toward us. It erodes your self esteem, and is unhealthy. Spend time with people that see you and value you for who you are. They end up becoming "wind beneath your wings," and truly making you feel as though you can accomplish anything.

10. Finish what you start. Something motivated you to start that project, whether it's the demand of the boss at work, or the need to freshen up your home. It could also be an exercise program. Once you find the motivation to start something, realize there will be obstacles that may get in your way. Each time you overcome that obstacle, you develop a deeper sense of accomplishment, which fuels your self esteem. It is a great feeling to start something, and it's an incredible feeling to finish it. Cross your finish line!

11. Focus on your personal gifts. All of us were created with unique gifts. We ALL have something we are really good at. Get in touch with your gift, and focus on that in your day to day living. Sometimes we get caught up in comparing ourselves to others, and if they happen to be better at something it erodes our self esteem. You are your own unique you. Find what makes you special and zone in on that. As you focus in on what you are naturally good at, again, your self esteem will sky rocket! You will feel happier and more productive in your life!

12. Take Action. Resolve to become intensely action oriented. Whenever you get a good idea or something needs to be done, move quickly.

Which book(s) will you begin reading?

How many pages per day?

Which food(s) can you add in to your diet to improve your energy and health?

What fitness activity will you add to increase your energy and production?

What tool will you utilize to maintain an even keel mood?

Which project will you stop putting off and complete?

THE RIGHT ATTITUDE

If you want to be truly successful in how you achieve your goals, then you need to have the right habits and attitudes that will keep you on track. There are a number of good traits you have to keep for life to discover that more opportunities and good things are bound to happen, if only you allow these.

1. Discipline and Consistency. Discipline is what separates the leaders from the followers. If you truly want to make changes in your life, you have to understand doing things even if you do not want to at times, and maintaining excellent quality and optimum performance each time. Being consistent is intertwined with patience, wherein you continue performing well, regardless of the situations and hindrances, to render the results you want in the end. Discipline and consistency are also interrelated, in the sense that discipline breeds consistency. If you continue practicing good habits; if you stick to the functions that lead to your main goal, you will find it easier to do over time. You will change as an entire person and experience the opportunities that come with being dedicated.

2. Resilience Problems are a part of every man's life, but it is the resilient person who always prevails and achieves their goals. You need to learn from your past mistakes and convert these into more productive actions the next time. Learn to pick yourself up after each fall and put in double effort to become better. Some of the most successful people, as well as those who truly left a mark in history, are known to have faced big difficulties

3. Optimism You need to stay positive about your situation, regardless of the problems that you face. It is vital that you stay optimistic and always believe that you will get to your goal, no matter what. If you tell yourself that you will reach it sooner, chances are you will.

4. Patience. Some goals are very big and will take time to accomplish. Do not allow yourself to think that some goals are just too huge to be possible. Be specific and set goals that are attainable to your current situation and start working to achieve these. You can break it down into smaller tasks that are much easier to do within the given time frame.

5. Effort. Here are some of the features that great people had. Hard work always pays off. Effort means working harder than anyone else, studying more than anyone else, and even suffering more than anyone else. You have to understand the importance of delayed gratification as you work towards your ultimate goal. To begin hard work, you can begin by fixing your schedule, writing down tasks and functions of the day, and finding the right people and resources that can assist you. Keep in mind that you have to be as independent as possible to finish more in the long term.

How are you open to opportunities today?

How will you overcome your obstacles today?

Are you being optimistic and patient?

Are you working diligently and consistently today?

WHAT SUCCESSFUL PEOPLE DO DIFFERENTLY

The people that seem to "have it all together" in fact DO. If you are looking for consistency in your results, then develop these habits for success. Take notice that not one of these is a "quick fix" or a "magic bullet". *Long-term achievement takes long-term planning and effort.*

1. Get Specific Goals. When you set a goal, try to be as specific as possible. "Lose 5 pounds" is a better goal than "lose some weight," because it gives you a clear idea of what success looks like. "Increase my income by $10,000" is better than "make more money". Knowing exactly what you want to achieve keeps you motivated until you get there. Also, think about the specific actions that need to be taken to reach your goal. Just promising that you will "eat less" or "sleep more" is too vague — be clear and precise. "I'll be in bed by 10pm on weeknights" leaves no room for doubt about what you need to do, and whether or not you have actually done it. *Vague goals beget vague results.*

2. Act on your goals. Given how busy most of us are, and how many goals we are juggling at once, it's not surprising that we routinely miss opportunities to act on a goal because we simply fail to notice them. Did you really have no time to work out today? No chance at any point to return that business phone call? Achieving your goal means grabbing hold of these opportunities before they slip through your fingers. Minimizing or eliminating the "should haves" and turning them into the "I did" is imperative to your improvement.

To seize the moment, decide when and where you will take action in advance. Again, be as specific as possible (e.g., "If it's Monday, Wednesday, or Friday, I'll work out for 30 minutes before work.") Studies show that this kind of planning will help your brain to detect and seize the opportunity when it arises, increasing your chances of success by roughly 300%.

3. Know exactly how far you have left to go. Achieving any goal also requires honest and regular monitoring of your progress — if not by others, then by you yourself. If you don't know how well you are doing, you can't adjust your behavior or your strategies accordingly. Check your progress frequently — weekly, or even daily, depending on the goal.

4. Be a realistic optimist. When you are setting a goal, engage in positive thinking about how likely you are to achieve it. Believing in your ability to succeed is enormously helpful for creating and sustaining your motivation. But whatever you do, don't underestimate how difficult it will be to reach your goal. Most goals worth achieving require time, planning, effort, and persistence. Studies show that thinking things will come to you easily and effortlessly leaves you ill-prepared for the journey ahead, and significantly increases the odds of failure. *Simple DOES NOT mean easy.*

5. Focus on getting better, rather than striving to be perfect. Believing you have the ability to reach your goals is important, but so is believing you can *get* the ability. Many of us believe that our intelligence, our personality, and our physical aptitudes are fixed — that no matter what we do, we won't improve. As a result, we focus on goals that are all about proving ourselves, rather than developing and acquiring new skills.

Fortunately, decades of research suggest that the belief in fixed ability is completely wrong — abilities of all kinds are profoundly malleable. Embracing the fact that you can change will allow you to make better choices, and reach your fullest potential. People whose goals are about getting better, rather than being good, take difficulty in stride, and appreciate the journey as much as the destination. *You can acquire whatever skills are necessary for you to succeed.*

5A. Take responsibility for your choices. Above all else, when you take responsibility for your choices, action s, and outcomes, Iit gives you power. You control your thoughts, you control your actions. You control your outcomes. If you have not been receiving the desired outcomes then it is time to stand tall and alter your thinking and strategies to make different choices.

Abraham Lincoln said "Because one man can is proof enough that all men can." *Effort, planning, persistence, and good strategies are what it really takes to succeed.* Embracing this knowledge will not only help you see yourself and your goals more accurately, but also do wonders for your outlook.

Taking responsibility means that you stop blaming others and circumstances for your setbacks and failures. It is the choices you have made that brought you where you are today, and the choices you make today determine where you'll be tomorrow. Choose to find a solution in every problem you face, rather than finding a problem in every solution.

6. Be determined. Determination is a willingness to commit to long-term goals, and to persist in the face of difficulty. The good news is if you aren't particularly determined now, there is something you can do about it. People who lack determination more often than not believe that they just don't have the innate abilities successful people have. If that describes your thinking there's no way to put this nicely: you are wrong. As I mentioned earlier, effort, planning, persistence, and good strategies are what it really takes to succeed. *Setbacks will inevitably occur. Persist and you will succeed.*

7. Build your willpower muscle. Your self-control "muscle" is just like the other muscles in your body — when it doesn't get much exercise, it becomes weaker over time. But when you give it regular workouts by putting it to good use, it will grow stronger and stronger, and better able to help you successfully reach your goals.

To build willpower, take on a challenge that requires you to do something you'd honestly rather not do. Give up high-fat snacks, do 100 squats a day, stand up straight when you catch yourself slouching, save $5.00 each day in cash safe or learn a new skill from reading or speaking with a mentor. When you find yourself wanting to give in, give up, or just not bother — don't. Start with just one activity, and make a plan for how you will deal with troubles when they occur ("If I have a craving for a snack, I will eat one piece of fresh fruit.") It will be hard in the beginning, but it will get easier, and that's the whole point. As your strength grows, you can take on more challenges and step-up your self-control workout.

8. Don't tempt fate. No matter how strong your willpower muscle becomes, it's important to always respect the fact that it is limited, and if you overtax it you will temporarily run out of steam. Don't try to take on two challenging tasks at once, if you can help it (like quitting smoking and dieting at the same time). And don't put yourself in harm's way — many people are overly-confident in their ability to resist temptation, and as a result they put themselves in situations where temptations abound. Successful people know not to make reaching a goal harder than it already is.

9. Focus on what you *will* do, not on what you will not do. Do you want to successfully lose weight, quit smoking, save money or put a lid on your bad temper? Then plan how you will replace bad habits with good ones, rather than focusing only on the bad habits themselves. Research on thought suppression (e.g., "Don't think about purple cows!") has shown that trying to avoid a thought makes it even more active in your mind. The same holds true when it comes to behavior — by trying not to engage in a bad habit, our habits get strengthened rather than broken.

If you want to change your ways, ask yourself, what will I do instead? For example, if you are trying to gain control of your temper you might make a plan like "If I am starting to feel angry, then I will take three deep breaths and count to 10 to calm down." By using deep breathing as a replacement for giving in to your anger, your bad habit will get worn away over time until it disappears completely.

10. Be decisive. Decisiveness is one of the most important qualities of successful and happy men and women, and decisiveness is developed through practice and repetition, over and over again until it becomes as natural to you as breathing in and breathing out.

EPIC!

TRAITS OF SUCCESSFUL PEOPLE

1. They are hard working. There is no such thing as easy money. Success takes hard work and people who are willing to do it. Successful people realize the sacrifices that they must make in order to achieve the results they truly desire.

2. They are honest. Those who are successful long-term are the honest ones. Successful people are honest with themselves regarding their strengths, needs, opportunities, and true production. Successful people realize that lying only delays results.

3. They persevere. How many success stories will go untold because they never happened? And all because someone quit. Successful people outlast everybody else. Successful people prepare for the hurdles to come, accept that there will be hurdles, plan for the ones they know will arise, and plan to overcome the unforeseen hurdles.

4. They are friendly. Have you noticed that most successful people are friendly and people oriented? This endears them to others and enables them to lead others to accomplish the task.

5. They are lifelong learners. Successful people are people who stretch themselves and grow continually, learning from all areas of life, including from their mistakes. Successful people surround themselves with people that will support and challenge them. They will seek out advice and education from the people they admire.

They are incredibly **curious** and eager. They study, ask questions, read constantly and apply what they learn. Repeated success is not about memorizing facts, it's about being able to take information and create, build, or apply it in new and important ways. Successful people want to learn everything about everything.

Let your mind be the sponge it was created to be – commit to learn something new every day. Read a book and/or watch an entertaining and educational TV show.

6. They over-deliver. The old statement of under-promise and over-deliver became famous because it made a lot of people successful.

7. They are Positive. Successful people do not allow themselves to be dragged down by small problems. They realize that life is filled with challenges, that there is good, bad and ugly that occurs to everyone in differing amounts at different times. Successful people put negativity in perspective and rebound quickly from setbacks.

8. They seek solutions in the face of problems. Problems are opportunities to do the impossible, not just complain. Successful people are the ones who find solutions. Successful people do not view the issue/obstacle as the end. They are solution based and action oriented.

9. They are creative. Successful people have a "Why not?" mentality. They see new combinations, new possibilities, new opportunities and challenges where others see problems or limitations. They wake up in the middle of the night yelling, "I've got it!" They ask for advice, try things out, and consult experts and amateurs, always looking for a better, faster, cheaper solutions. Successful people create stuff!

10. They are self-reliant and take responsibility. Successful people don't worry about blame, and they don't waste time complaining. They make decisions and move on. Successful people take the initiative and accept the responsibilities of success.

11. They are usually relaxed and keep their perspective. Even in times of stress, successful people keep their balance; they know the value of timing, humor, and patience. They rarely panic or make decisions on impulse. Successful people breath easily, ask the right questions, and make sound decisions, even in a crisis.

12. They live in the present moment. They know that "Now" is the only time they can control. They have a "gift" for looking people in the eye, listening to what is being said - they hardly ever seem rushed, and they get a lot done! They take full advantage of each day. Successful people don't waste time, they use it!

13. They seek assistance when it is needed. The most successful people I know seek out the guidance of a coach to get a different perspective, ask the right questions, and aid them in getting "un-stuck".

14. They are grateful. Having an attitude of gratitude invites even better things to come into your life. Life cannot be fun if you are angry and emotional all of the time.

15. They embrace change. It's impossible to reach your full potential if you're not willing to change. Come to the realization that change is good!

16. They BRING IT ALL. EVERYDAY. Successful people do more and give more than the average person. Successful people have set goals and have created a plan to achieve them. Successful people wake up and TAKE ACTION.

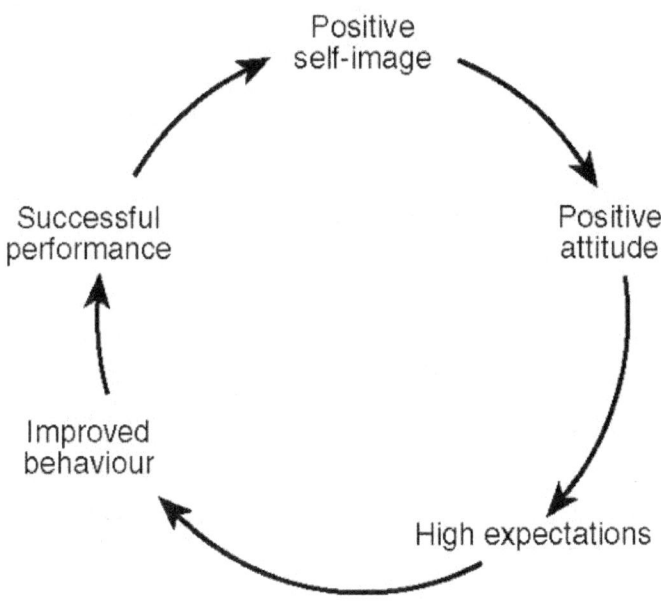

STAYING MOTIVATED

If you lack motivation, there is good cause for it - you have impotent goals. This means you either do not know what you want, or that what you want does not put fire in your soul.

Getting motivated comes from taking action on your goals. Many individuals wait for motivation to take action. It actually works the opposite way. Prolonged motivation comes from knowing exactly what you are achieving and why. Use these tools to get and stay motivated.

1. Visualize what you want. Picture yourself attaining the goal you want to achieve. Some of us see still pictures, and others see moving pictures (like a movie). Some of us see our pictures or movies in color, and others see them in black and white. However it is important that you see your picture, and get in tuned to the details of the picture.

2. Use all of your senses when visualizing. As you visualize, start to pay attention to the sounds associated with your picture. Also, notice how you feel in that picture. This feeling should be both emotional and physical. How does your body feel fitting back into those skinny jeans? How does that make you feel, emotionally? The more details you have in your picture, the more you are sending a message to your brain that this is really happening. Before you know it, it really happens.

3. Write down your goals. Writing down your goals is a great way to stay focused on what you want. You can place your goals where you see them daily. Some people also just like to write their goals then put them away. That's fun, because when you go back weeks, month, or even years later and read your goals, you are amazed at what you have accomplished.

 4. Believe in your goals. Choose goals that you truly believe in your heart that you will attain. Understand, as humans, we tend to send ourselves "doubting messages" when we think of goals we want. Acknowledge what that is - just doubt - and mentally set it aside. Think about what you want. Believe in yourself and in your goal. Strive for it, one step at a time.

5. Challenge yourself. Choose goals that you know in your heart you can attain. With that, make sure you are challenging yourself. It's that stretching moment in our lives that keep us motivated. It tough to be challenged, yet it feels great! Just to know you're always stretching to go a little further is motivating in itself. It keeps you from getting bored and stagnant.

6. Get support. Tell those that love and care for you about your goals. Simply talking about it will motivate you (as well as inspire them). They can hold you accountable, encourage you, and celebrate with you.

7. Strive for continued progress. As you accomplish each goal, replace it with a new goal that will push you to another level. This goes back to keeping yourself challenged, and avoiding boredom. When we find ourselves at a stagnant place in our lives, we tend to start to go backwards. Always give yourself something for which to strive.

8. Reward yourself for accomplishments. To stay motivated, give yourself a reward for what you have accomplished. This moment of celebration is so important. It's called positive reinforcement, and it feels so good that you want to set another goal and celebrate it again. Rewards can be anywhere from a pat on the back to a week-long vacation.

Who is your positive support system?

Who is your negative support system?

What challenges will you overcome this week?

How will you reward yourself for your accomplishments?

GET THINGS DONE

If constantly putting tasks off till later is causing you stress and consistently making you feel disappointed in yourself, then here are a few tips to help you to stop procrastination in its tracks once and for all!

1. Causes of Procrastination

Identifying the causes of procrastination is the first step in overcoming procrastination.

You've probably resolved to make a change, but once again you find yourself in familiar territory of leaving things till the last minute.

2. Procrastination has the potential to rob you of your potential.

Is procrastination:

- causing you stress
- reducing the quality of your work
- souring your relationships with colleagues and family?

If so, then it is time to act.

3. Procrastination is not about a lack of willpower!

Psychologists have identified a number of causes of procrastination. These include:

- a lack of clear goals
- indecision
- fear of failure
- anger and resentment
- feeling overwhelmed
- fatigued or tired.

4. So, how do we overcome our obstacles and keep moving forward?

1. Determine the areas of your life that are suffering the most not taking action and then list every *benefit* you believe you will experience as a result of doing what you know you should do.

Identify the *consequences* of not taking action. What is the most painful result of not getting started on the thing you've been avoiding? When the pain of not doing something exceeds the pain of doing it, it's likely to get done. Whenever you avoid doing what should be done, you do so for a reason; there are some benefits. Ask yourself, "What are the benefits of my not taking action?" One of the benefits could be that you spare yourself the pain and effort of changing. It is important to acknowledge this. It is only after facing our reasons for inaction that we can say to ourselves, "I don't have to run away from my problems any longer because I'm big enough and strong enough to take it. This exercise is to break the tie with an emotional reaction and form the habit of acting rationally.

Write a list of every action step you need to take in order to complete a task or project. Put a deadline to it and DO IT!

2. Do the unpleasant stuff first. One of the reasons we put off certain tasks is because some aspect of them is unpleasant; for example we may need to make a difficult telephone call or perform our least favorite chore. Write down the worst tasks which need doing each day and make sure you do them first. Try not to think about it too much, you may find that the most unpleasant tasks often turn out to be a lot easier than you think once you take action. Give yourself a little reward when you have completed them.
Once these are out the way, you will feel more motivated to tackle the easier stuff on your list.

3. Do a cost-benefit analysis. Compare the pain of acting now with the pain you will feel in the future if you do not act. Which pain is more severe? Choose to accept a LITTLE pain now for BIG rewards in the future. Focus on what you want (the benefits of acting), not on what you don't want (the pain of changing).

Follow your current behavior to its logical long-term conclusion. What is the worst case scenario? Instead of avoiding the pain, face it and amplify it! The purpose of this exercise is to get your emotions working for you, rather than against you. All you need is to accept your feelings and act despite them. In other words, say to yourself something like, "I don't feel like acting now, but some things are more important than my feelings. For example, my success and happiness are more important than my reluctance to act. So, despite how I feel now, I'm going to do what's best for me. After all, I deserve to be successful and happy."

4. Sometimes we procrastinate because we lack focus and direction of what needs to be done. Make a list of what tasks need to be completed each day, and prioritize them in order of importance (or unpleasantness!). Commit to starting and finishing the first item on the list before moving to the next. Make a step by step plan for each task, and commit yourself to completing one step at a time.

5. The task appears too big. Any task which appears to be too big can cause us to procrastinate, as we can feel overwhelmed by it, such as clearing your whole house, or starting a business. The best way of dealing with this is to break each task down into smaller, more manageable steps. For the house clearance example, you may decide to start with one room, or an area of one room. If the task is starting your own business you may set yourself smaller tasks such as spending time researching your business idea, then working on acquiring skills you may need.

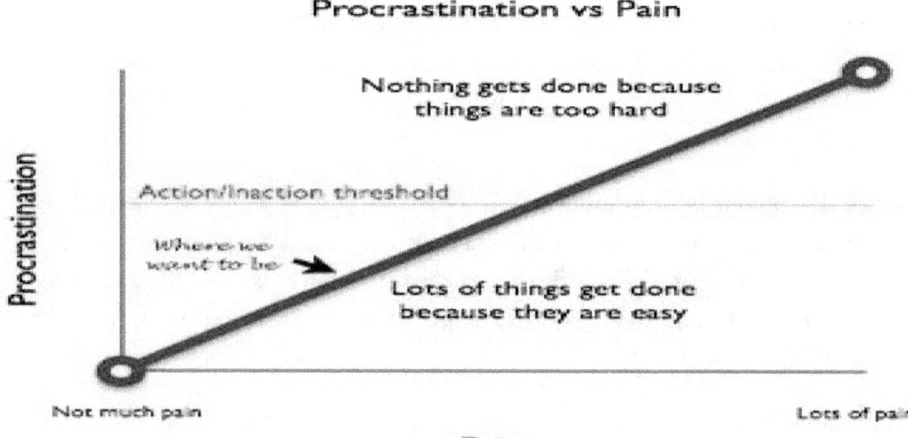

Procrastination vs Pain

Nothing gets done because things are too hard

Action/inaction threshold

Where we want to be

Lots of things get done because they are easy

Procrastination

Not much pain

Lots of pain

Pain

REBOUNDING FROM FAILURES

What separates people who enjoy success from the majority who end up never getting what they want is how we respond to failure. It is what we do about failure that makes a big difference.

There are three ways in which people respond to failure.

1. Give Excuses, Lay Blame & Give up. What do some people do when they don't get what they want? They will start making excuses and blame everything and everyone around them. They say things like, 'it's not fair', 'I'm just not smart enough' 'It's just too difficult', 'I'm too young' or 'I'm too old', 'I just didn't have the luck', 'the depressed economy affected me'.

Feeling helpless and frustrated, this first group will stop taking action and give up! They will resign themselves to their goal being out of reach and live a life of mediocrity.

2. Keep Trying the Same thing Over and Over Again. These are the people who have a lot more determination than the first. When they don't get their outcome, they will not quit. They will get themselves to take action again. The motto of this group is, 'I failed because I did not try hard enough' 'If I keep trying, I will eventually succeed'. So they keep taking action, putting in more time, energy and effort. No matter how many times they fail, they just keep trying harder and harder.

Will they eventually achieve their goals? It depends. If they set small, incremental goals, they may, with enough time and efforts eventually succeed. However, if they set big and exceptional goals, like becoming the top in their field, they will never be successful by just trying again and again. They may experience a better result, but they won't reach the goals they desire. Why?

Although they keep taking action, they do not change their strategy. If you keep using the same approach, you are going to keep getting the same result. I have seen so many professionals and businessmen repeat this limiting pattern.

I know many businessmen who fail in their business only to start again and do the same thing. They keep putting in ads that don't work, they hire ineffective people or they use the same business model.

3. Get Feedback, Change Strategy, and Take Action until you Succeed.
So what is the pattern that all successful individuals exhibit? When they don't achieve their goals, they don't think of it as failure. Instead, they perceive it as feedback. Either feedback that the strategy they used was ineffective or that they did not take enough action. They then use this feedback to immediately change their strategy and take action again.

If they still don't succeed, they will get more feedback, change their strategy, and take action again. They keep repeating this process until they get what they want. They do whatever it takes. So, remember, every time you don't get what you want, it is life giving you feedback. It is this continuous feedback you need to help you adjust your approach until you hit your target.

Thomas Edison took almost 10,000 attempts before inventing the light bulb. When asked how he did it, he said that he had to first find 9,999 strategies of how not to invent the light bulb. He then used this feedback to change his strategy until he got what he wanted.

Successful people review and change their strategy whenever they encounter 'failure'. They understand that failure is feedback. Understand this principle and you will overcome failure and achieve success in no time at all.

CHAPTER 2

TAKING CARE OF YOURSELF

Think Better, Eat Better, Move Better, Feel Better, Be Better

All of these components must be addressed to live a fit, healthy and High Performance life. Each component takes work and time to achieve. Simple does not mean easy, and effort in each is required. In the end, what you put into each will be what you get from it.

If you look at your path as a lifelong journey, your attitude toward change will focus on long-term and short-term success. This will inevitably enhance your results. At times you will need to give more attention and effort to each component of life.

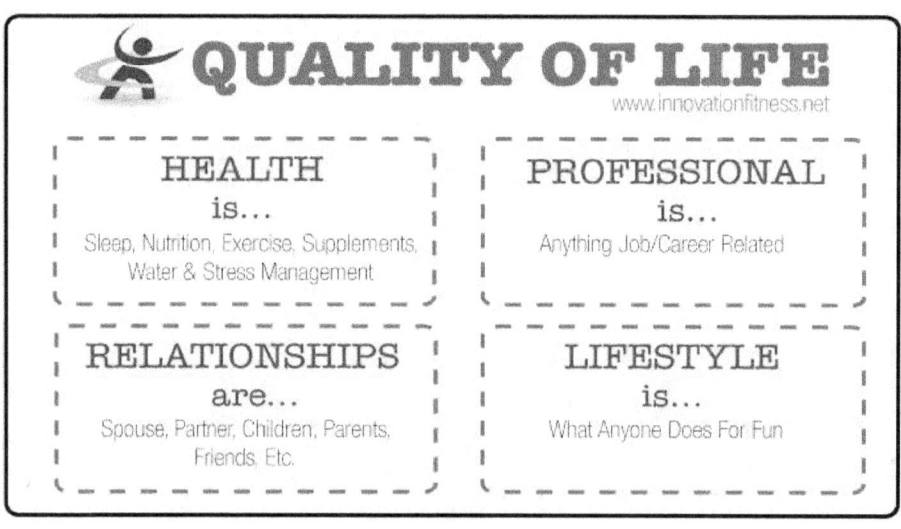

Each of these components can be broken down into smaller parts.

SETTING UP YOUR PERSONAL DEVELOPMENT PLAN

Think Better
Clarity, Planning, Focus and Control

1. Reason - Find your why. Why do you want to do that action? Is it to have fun? Do you wish to get in shape? To create financial security? To live a life dream? I have said for years that I want to run a 10k but all that talk never got me close because there was a bunch of training involved and I only cared about the finish line of the run. You need to know what will get you on the track, or in the class, or in the training field.

2. Goals - To act you need to know what you want. This is critical. If you are going to get involved, you need to know what action you want to take. Be clear in stating what you are achieving.

3. Plan - You have to make your schedule. If you do not make a schedule that is yours ,then you are giving up your power to something else. If you do not make a plan for yourself, then other peoples priorities will fill your days and nights for you.

> **Identify your Problem Areas –** What are your biggest Challenges? Different problems require different solutions. If you try to change everything at once, nothing will change.

> **Select Solutions –** Select up to three to five small changes you think will most easily and effectively enable you to address only your most troubling challenge. Be certain that these changes are R.P.M. changes. Always choose something you know you can repeat.

4. Execute Your Plan – Do not worry about the process, just the next step. If you look too far ahead, it becomes a giant mountain, not a bunch of fun. It is important to make these changes each day. There is power in consistency. One way to do this is to keep a calendar or keep a record to mark your daily progress. Tell your friends and family about the commitment you have made. Do other things you believe will help keep you on track, like wearing a wristband or other reminder, posting signs for yourself, writing a food diary, or joining a group that is committed to making the same kind of changes.

Action - Start everyday with action. This has nothing to do with individual goals of what you want to achieve but instead is an overall way to live life. You need to start every day with a few things that have to be done, have to be acted on and then no matter what you want, you can eventually finish them.

5. Measure – Review you successes and failures regularly. Do not stress about your past, simply begin at the REASON again and get going. You cannot change past (in)actions but you can act now. I have never met anyone that has done everything perfectly. Just keep strategically moving forward.

Revisit Each Month – Your actions and needs will change over time, and so should your plan. If you have successfully turned all three (or even one) of your changes into a new habit, you can move on and tackle a new problem. Make sure that your plan changes along with you. Changes are intended to last you a lifetime, so they need to evolve.

6. Results – Do this for 90 days and you will be on the path to lasting change. Do this for a year and you will be astonished by your accomplishments. When you do, it is time to celebrate, because you have not been "dieting," you have started to break the bad habits that caused a lifetime of overeating, and under moving. You will be on your way to freedom from all of the frustration and confusion and on the path to being healthy and fit.

Use the following questions to organize your thoughts and set your mind straight.

1. Do you have a weight problem, tried every diet but none of them have worked?

2. Do you smoke and want to quit?

3. Do you get down on yourself when you do not do things perfectly?

4. Do you see the positive or the negative side of a situation?

5. Do you smile often and genuinely?

6. Do you laugh a lot?

7. Do you make excuses, justifications, and promises to yourself to "do it tomorrow"?

8. Does tomorrow ever come? It is time. Tomorrow is here. It IS time for a change.

9. What change will you make in your attitude this week?

10. What change will you make in your food choices this week?

11. What change will you make in your fitness level this week?

Eat Better

Nutrition and Weight Management Components to maximize performance.

Eating better requires understanding the building blocks of nutrition and ignoring fad diets hyped by the mainstream media. Ignoring "magical" supplements and focusing on better habits will enable you to perform at your best. Choose to eat according to your needs and values.
You can eat anything you want. You just cannot eat EVERYTHING that you want whenever you want.

Here are a few suggestions on Eating better for life:
- Make "Better Bad Food Choices" whenever possible
- Eat Breakfast
- Eat Balanced Meals (Pro, Carbohydrate, Fat)
- Eat Consistently throughout the day (avoid missing meals)
- Stay Hydrated
- Nutritional Insurance by using a Multi Vitamin
- Enjoy life's pleasures in moderation
- Eat according to goals and values
- Eat to provide as much health as you find acceptable
- Intentionally add fruits and vegetables to your meals
- Cook large – Package small
- Experiment with new, healthy recipes
- Maintain a consistent diet on weekends and weekdays
- Track food intake
- Plan meals on most days of the week
- Track fat and calories
- Measure food at least 2 days per week
- Control your portion size
- Trim Fat
- Distance Yourself from Tempting Foods
- Make Smart Choices at Restaurants
- Embrace Fruits and Veggies. Add them to your daily menu
- Downsize Your Dinnerware
- Don't let yourself get too hungry
- Move Throughout the Day
- Track Your Progress
- Fill Up with Fiber

Eating Habits Assessment

1. Current eating habits?

Do you eat at desk?

Where and how do you eat the majority of your meals?

What do you eat during these times?

How will this be compatible with your new food choices?

2. Are you prepared to eat differently than your friends at social functions?

Eating often accompanies many social gatherings. How do your friends eat?
Do they consume foods that you know will not be compatible with your lifestyle?

How will you address this?

3. Are you prepared to change your home environment?

Does your home environment work with your new plans? You may have chosen to eat mindfully and leisurely. The trouble is your home is utterly chaotic, noisy, and messy, with barely a place to sit down, let alone have a large pleasant space to indulge in your new meals.

What will you do to change this?

4. How do your current habits fit?

What if your leisure activities always involve eating junk food?

What happens if you start a diet that completely rules out junk food?

What will you do? Change your habits? Find a different comfort food?

5. What about eating away from home?

Do you eat at restaurants a lot?

Which restaurants do you go to?

Will they fit with your new style of eating?

Are you prepared to leave food on your plate if their portions are too big?

6. Is your kitchen set-up properly?

Take a look around your kitchen.

Do you actually have enough fridge/freezer space?

Enough containers? Enough time?

7. Are you being totally honest with yourself?

You read about a new diet in a magazine, and it requires eating a lot more vegetables. On the surface you are busting to lose "10 pounds in 2 weeks", but deep down you know you cannot stand vegetables. Which part of you will win out in the end?

Why do you hate veggies? Are you prepared to cook more, or learn different ways of cooking them?

8. Can you accept the things you cannot change?
You cannot change the way other people act and the way they speak - "oh, so you're on another health kick again are you?" But you can choose ahead of time how you will respond inwardly and outwardly .

9. Will you continue monitoring yourself objectively?
Many people reach their ideal weight, and then let old habits creep back in. However there are a few warning systems in place. One is the waistband in your pants. Will you choose to conveniently ignore it if it gets tighter? Or will you be objective?

10. How will the lifestyle of family and friends affect your health/weight loss efforts?
If your whole world is filled with people who are couch potatoes, how do you plan to work against this culture? Will they influence you to be more active or more sedentary?

Becoming aware of what, when, how and why you eat can help to lose weight

Get Motivated — Get Educated
Take Control — Get Results
www.InnovationFitness.net

Slow down - Remember to be mindful about your food choices and eating habits.
Be patient with yourself - Changing behaviors is a long process, but it is also long-lasting.
Expect to slip up - Don't even entertain the idea of perfection. If there were no mistakes, there'd be nothing to learn from. If you "blow it" today, make a plan for tomorrow that includes solutions to the difficulties.
Determine your overeating cues - If you're overeating often – you're just putting a band-aid on a gaping wound. Try to determine the root cause of what's eating you by following the recommendations above.
Motivation follows action - That is, getting motivated to change your eating patterns isn't going to hit you someday. You must act first. When you see results, you will be motivated to continue. **NUTRITION MARKERS**

You can do this! Believe in yourself today!

Targets

Fiber –	25+ grams per day
Water –	Bodyweight X .75 =
Sodium -	<2400 MG
Fat -	<30% TCI or =/< 600 calories
Protein -	Bodyweight X .75
Energy –	6+
Meal Timing –	3 -5 hours

Move Better

Life doesn't need to be complex and neither does improving your High Performance Lifestyle through improved health, increased fitness, and weight loss. Many people I have met struggle with consistent exercise. They have an improper or sour mindset about "Fitness". Many believing that they must belong to a Fitness Center and do long, hard workouts everyday to see results. Or, they believe that while there, everybody knows what they're doing except for them. The good news is that better fitness can be achieved anywhere.

Here are very simple steps to take to look and feel great:

1. **MOVE X's 5**

    Move: Just Do Something

    Move More: Aim for a minimum of 100 minutes of 'Huffy Puffy' exercise every week

    Move More Often: Aim to do something everyday

    Move Quicker: Aim to go faster over the same distance or further in the same time

    Move Differently: Choose different activities or do the same activity differently. E.g. run or walk a different way every day, run hills, flat, sand, slower for longer and shorter and quicker

2. **Commit to take the path of MOST resistance.** Escalators and elevators are a friend to weight gain and low performance. Remember Newton's law of motion – An object in motion stays in motion. An object at rest stays at rest. You are the object. If you begin your day moving you will stay moving. If you begin your day with the habit of inactivity it is that much harder to get motivated to move.

3. **Surprise Exercise.** Look for opportunities to move where you would not normally. Take a phone call while standing, pace during a conference call, set your laptop high so you can stand and work, take the furthest parking spot every time.

4. Make Exercise a non-negotiable priority. We do what is important to us. Know that exercise/movement aids in reducing pains, increasing metabolism, creating sustained energy, and makes us feel better. Do not accept not exercising.

Fitness and Exercise Components:

Moving better requires several interconnected parts. Each of these is important to creating success in your exercise program.

Cardiovascular conditioning—Your heart is the second most important organ (after the brain) and needs to be conditioned to achieve fitness success. The right cardio program can help you burn calories more efficiently while keeping you fit for increased activity.

Flexibility—Your body needs to move efficiently. Overactive or underactive muscles can influence how you move, potentially leading to injuries. Therefore, you need to maintain proper posture and flexibility while you train.

Core training—Your core is made up of your abdominals, low back, and hips. It needs to be trained to keep you strong from the inside out and create better movement patterns for the arms and legs.

Balance training—Balance means being able to control your body during movement. In other words, training your body to control unwanted movement that might throw you off-base helps you avoid falls and unwanted injuries throughout your life.

Resistance training—Keeping your body strong and increasing lean muscle mass are all integral to living a fit life. Resistance training is a key component of all of the above. The more muscle you have, the higher your metabolism, the lower your body fat percentage is, and the more you can do.

Each small working part has a role in overall fitness and must be trained accordingly. A healthy and fit lifestyle will encompass all the larger components as well as the smaller, moving parts.

MOVEMENT TIPS

1. Tune in to an audio book while you walk. It will keep you going longer and looking forward to the next walk—and the next chapter! Check your local library for a great selection. Look for a whodunit; you might walk so far you will need to take a cab home!

2. Drinking too little water can hamper your weight loss efforts and your ability to think clearly. That is because dehydration can slow your metabolism by 3 percent, or about 45 fewer calories burned a day, which in a year could mean weighing 5 pounds more. The key to water is not only how much you drink, it is how frequently you drink it. Small amounts sipped often work better than 8 ounces gulped down at once.

3. Exercise burns calories and keeps your muscles strong, so choose a combination of cardiovascular training and resistance exercises. You can join a health club, or buy a few fitness DVDs and set up your own workout room at home. I think the best part about exercising is how good your body feels as you get stronger. Moreover, when your body feels good, you are going to be more motivated to take care of yourself by eating right.

4. Building muscle strength and endurance through exercise will increase your total body strength and help you to maintain good posture.

This exercise for the backs of your legs can be done in front of the television! Sit up straight with your legs, feet, and knees hip width apart. Keeping the weight evenly distributed between both feet lift your heels off the floor. Place your palms on your thighs with your elbows bent and push down as though you are trying to push your heels back onto the floor. Resist this movement with your legs. Once you have mastered this lean forward and upwards slightly to add weight.

Stair climbers are excellent machines for cardiovascular conditioning. They are not intended for strength training and, contrary to rumors ,will not give you big muscles or make your butt big.

Lunges are awesome lower body workouts. Beginners to these lower body exercises should do them without weights. Once you get stronger lunges can be done while holding dumbbells in your hands to add resistance. Start by standing with your feet together. Take a long step forward with one foot. Come down with your heel first. Then bend your front leg and sink down so the knee on your back leg is a few inches off the floor. Do not let the knee on your forward leg go past your toes or drift to either side.

Step up to the plate, work your thighs, and butt! Step-ups are good leg strengthening lower body exercises you can do at home or at the gym. Find a sturdy step, bench, or box that is just lower than your knee so when you put your foot on it your thigh will be parallel to the ground. If it is higher, it will be hard on your knee. Too much lower and it will not be effective. Have a support you can hold on to with one hand to steady yourself during your lower body workouts.

Here is a good lower body exercise for the hip abductor, which is the muscle on the outside of your hip that moves your leg out to the side. It is one of the best exercises to tone lower body muscles. Stand on a stair step sideways with one foot on the step. Without bending the supporting leg, lower the unsupported leg a couple of inches by tilting your pelvis and then bring it back up. Repeat ten times and switch to the other leg.

5. When you stretch your body in preparation for exercise as well as after exercise, you need to stretch your mind as well. You might be wondering how and why. When your mind is relaxed, your body follows. To achieve a relaxed mind listen to soothing music, relax your breathing, and use visualization techniques such as imagining the most peaceful place you can think of.

6. Weekend workouts are not enough! Do not just save all your exercise plans for the weekend. Regular exercise throughout the week will build up your muscles slowly as well as your endurance. Vigorous exercise done only occasionally can lead to torn or strained tissue and will not do much to improve your looks or sports performance either.

7. Turn your household chores into a fitness challenge. Sweep or mop using as much energy as possible and exaggerate your arm movements. Fold your clothes and do a couple sets of squats at the same time. You might as well get fit while you make your parents happy. Just be sure the blinds are closed to prevent embarrassing moments!

8. To boost your metabolism and burn more calories consider alternating between two different kinds of exercise rather than just sticking to one. Try running one day and strength training or swimming on another.

9. The best thing about aerobic exercise is that the benefits are cumulative. You essentially gain the same health benefits from taking three ten-minute walks throughout the day as you do from taking one 30 minute walk. With this in mind, it can be much easier to break your activity goal into manageable pieces that will fit into your day.

10. Want to get fit faster? Then keep moving and be active. Just walking up the stairs when you have the chance instead of taking the escalator can make a difference. By constantly moving you are burning fat and keeping your metabolism revved.

Being active is the enemy of unwanted weight. If you are not active and not doing anything you may just reach out for food to kill boredom.

Regular physical activity reduces the risk for many diseases, helps control weight, and strengthens muscles, bones, and joints.

Walking is awesome exercise. Any place you can walk uninterrupted and build up a brisk pace is good. In the mall walking for exercise is more fun when you are window shopping!

Exercise is great but you have to watch what you eat in order to get the best results from your workouts. Working out in the gym in order to lose fat while paying no attention to what you eat is like trying to save money while charging up your credit card.

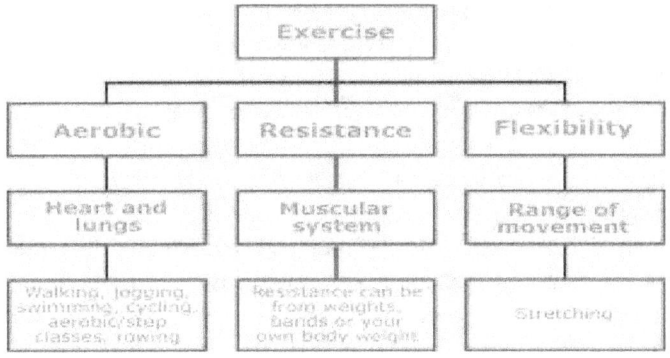

FEEL BETTER

Feeling better requires the understanding that we are our biggest asset or that we can be our biggest liability. Being Proactive and consistently doing the things that make you feel good about yourself, rather than reactive actions that temporarily make us feel good will allow us to make strides towards Feeling Better.

When you begin to incorporate the strategies from the Think, Move and Eat Better categories you will begin to feel and see changes in your daily routine. These changes are all positive and will have a cumulative effect on your happiness.

Taking care of your body and taking care of your mind by providing positive support will create less negative stress, more feelings of accomplishment, better ability to focus, and an increased ability to perform due to increased energy and drive.

- Increased Mobility
- Enhanced Mental Focus
- Increased Energy and Drive
- Better Decision Making and Problem Solving
- Proactive Actions that are Goal and Value Driven
- Decreased Stress

"Promise Yourself"

To be so strong that nothing disturbs your peace of mind.

To talk Health, happiness, and prosperity to every person you meet.

To make all of your friends feel that there is something worthwhile in them.

To look at the sunny side of everything and make your optimism come true.

To think only the best, to work only for the best and to expect only the best.

To be just as enthusiastic about the success of others as you are about your own.

To forget the mistakes of the past and press on to the greater achievements of the future.

To wear a cheerful expression at all times and give a smile to every living creature that you meet.

To give so much time to improving yourself that you have no time to criticize others.

To be too large to worry, too noble for anger, too strong for fear, and too happy to permit the presence of trouble.

To think well of yourself and to proclaim this fact to the world, not in loud word, but in great deeds.

To live in the faith that the whole world is on your side, so long as you are true to the best that is in you.

TRANSFORM YOUR THINKING · TRANSFORM YOUR BODY · TRANSFORM YOUR LIFE

-Christian D. Larson   www.InnovationFitness.net

All stress isn't bad. Stress can initiate change, help us focus on the task at hand, and in some cases even save our lives. Yet, when stress builds up, it can result in the opposites— and cause us to spin our wheels, keep us from concentrating, and cause bodily injury and even loss of life.

The first tip in managing stress is to recognize your stressors. The next step is to put each of them in their place. The following stress management tips, based on some old and some new adages, can help you do just that!

Take a Deep Breath and Count to Ten—
Taking a deep breath or two adds oxygen to your system, which almost instantly helps you relax. In addition, taking a moment to step back can help you maintain your composure, which in the long run, is what you need to work rationally through a stressful situation.

Start with "take a deep breath" and…

1. Count to ten (or more or less as the situation warrants!)
2. Stand up and stretch. Remember relaxation is the opposite of stress.
3. Stand up and smile. Try it! You'll feel better!
4. Take a short walk. If you're at work, take a bathroom break or get a glass of water. Do something that changes your focus. When you come back to the problem, chances are it won't seem nearly as insurmountable.

"Things happen" and sometimes "bad things happen to good people". If we let them, stressful events can build up, wall us in, and eventually stop us from enjoying the good things in life.

1. **Take the time.** Too often we put the pleasantries of life on the back burner, telling ourselves we don't "have time" or can't "make time" for them. However, actually, time is the only thing we do completely own. While we can't "make" a day that's longer than 24 hours, each of us starts the day with exactly that amount of time. Take a part of your time to recognize the good things in your life.
2. **Sleep on it.** Every coin has two sides and every issue has both pros and cons. List them both then put the list away and take a second look tomorrow. Sometimes "sleeping on" a situation changes the minuses to pluses.
3. **Every cloud has a silver lining.** After all, rain makes things grow! Ben Franklin found good in a bolt of lightning. Find the good in your stressful situation by listing the negative surges and determining what it will take to make them into positive charges!

Know Your Limitations

Knowing yourself and your limits may be the most important way to manage stress effectively.

1. **Dare to say no.** One more little thing may be the "straw that breaks the camel's back". It's okay to say "No", "I can't", or "Later".
2. **Acquit yourself.** Sometimes events really are out of control and you really are "Not Guilty". Quit blaming yourself.
3. **When you need help, get help.** Even Atlas couldn't bear the weight of the world on his shoulders forever. Whether you need help from kids or spouse in hauling groceries into the house, help from a colleague to solve a work-related problem, or professional help to find the causes of and effectively manage your stress, getting the help you need is in itself a major stress management tip!

STRESS REDUCTION KIT
STRESS IS A KILLER.

Stress can create havoc and it creates a host of health trouble. Utilize these steps to gain back control.

To get out of feeling overwhelmed:

1. Acknowledge it.

2. Take a moment to breath.

3. Notice that of the things causing the feeling, some are more urgent or important than others.

4. Notice which elements you have control or influence over, and which ones you don't.

5. List some things that can be put off for now, or may not even be necessary.

6. Pick one thing to do right now. Doing one thing at a time is calming and is the most effective way to make progress.

SYMPTOMS OF STRESS

- Anxious
- Mind-racing
- Chest palpitations
- Problems concentrating
- Easily irritated
- Avoiding people and responsibilities
- Focusing on negative thoughts
- Anger issues
- Headaches
- Digestive problems
- Muscle tension and pain
- Sleep issues
- Fatigue
- High blood pressure
- Weight loss or gain
- Skin problems - breakouts, rashes, hives

STRESS RELIEF TIPS

- Eat right and exercise
- Set realistic goals
- Handle important tasks first and eliminate unessential tasks
- Take a break to slow down "mind-racing"
- Reduce the urge to be "perfect"
- Be flexible
- Avoid excessive competition
- Reduce criticism of yourself and others
- Don't stress when expectations are not met
- Manage your anger
- Push away negativity of any kind
- Give yourself "me" time
- Choose to keep quiet when you feel a negative reaction
- Be cheerful, it deflates other's stress
- Silence your phone at night
- Utilize relaxation techniques; Yoga, Meditation, Breathing, etc.
- Laugh and smile more often
- Remember you can only change yourself

BETTER SLEEP

1. **Learn the optimal hours you need to sleep:** Everyone is different. Genetics determine how much sleep a person needs. The key is to determine how many hours you need to sleep each night to feel refreshed in the morning. Some people need 5, 6 or 8 hours a night. Most people know the amount of hours that work best for them. Remember that number and set up your schedule to achieve those hours. This will allow your body to optimally function and prevent any sleep deficits.

2. **Create a dark environment:** Less light triggers increased Melatonin release (your sleep hormone), which allows the body to enter into a deeper quality of sleep.

3. **Create a quiet environment:** Noisy environments have been shown to interrupt sleep cycles.

4. **Sleep on a comfortable bed, pillow and sheets:** Comfort allows your muscles to relax and your body to stay in the proper alignment.

5. **Sleep schedule:** Create a schedule that allows each day to be similar with wake time and bed time. Keep the range plus or minus one hour.

6. **Write down all thoughts at least an hour before bed:** The mind seems to race at bedtime with thoughts of what to do the next day and life concerns. This happens to 90% of all clients we have worked with. The solution is making sure all thoughts are written down and dealt with at least one hour before bedtime.

7. **Create proper down time:** Many people work, watch TV, or exercise before bedtime. The mind needs to be prepared for sleep. The best recommendation is make sure at least an hour before bedtime you are beginning to relax and prepare your body for optimal sleep.
    A few examples:
    Taking a Bath
    Reading
    Light relaxing walk
    Listening to relaxing music

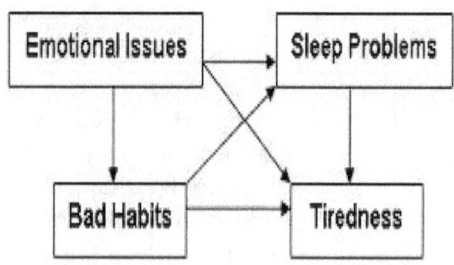

BE BETTER

Control, Consistency and Planning: A cumulative effect of your efforts.

"Being" better results from a deconstruction and reconstruction of your habits.

Treating yourself BETTER has an effect on all areas of your life. The most rewarding and successful changes come from learning to be your best asset, by becoming your "biggest cheerleader". Success in one area of Wellness tends to have a carryover effect into other areas. When you are feeling better and thinking better you will Be Better.

Finding positives in every circumstance, gaining the ability to continually move forward, having the belief in yourself that you can accomplish the previously not attempted or not accomplished and focusing on solutions, rather being mired down in issues or problems will make you Be Better.

"Grant me the STRENGTH to accept the things I cannot change; The Courage to change the things I can; and the Wisdom to know the difference is in me." – Modified Serenity Prayer - Nancy Wasson, PHD

What changes will you make to your eating habits?

Where can you add in more movement?

Which new tools will you utilize to reduce your stress?

Which new tools will you utilize for Time ~~Management~~ Effectiveness?

How many times will you choose to smile and laugh per day?

Signs of Success and Accomplishment

Being satisfied with your life	81%
Being in control of your life	79%
Having a good marriage	76%
Spending lots of time with your family	69%
Being spiritually fulfilled	65%
Having a balance between work and personal life	65%
Being physically fit	54%
Regularly donating your time to help others in need	52%
Being a leader in your community	34%
The only meaningful measure of success is money	14%

CHAPTER 3

THE BEST HEALTH AND LIFESTYLE HABITS OF SUCCESSFUL PEOPLE

Grab a highlighter and get to work.
Section by section. Point by point.
Choose the habits that you will implement for continued success.

Thought Process:

1. Make realistic (R.P.M.) commitments— Achieving anything more than what you have now will require realistic investments of your time, energy, and will power. Do not make promises you won't keep.

Visualize your success—See yourself as you want to be.
Mental imagery can provide numerous benefits, such as enhancing your belief in your abilities to achieve your goals.
See yourself look and act as the person you desire to be.

Remain Positive and Proactive – Just consider how futile negativity is. There is only a positive benefit to being positive.

Define success for yourself—Dig deep and discover what it means to you to be fit, healthy, happy and successful. Create smart goals.

Commit to get and stay fit— When you make a promise, especially to yourself, it is important to keep it. Dedication is important when you want to achieve a goal. Without commitment, fitness will always be something you want, not something you have.

2. Ask empowering questions. Instead of asking "Why is this happening to me?" ask yourself, "How will I benefit from this challenge? What is the hidden opportunity? What valuable lesson can I learn? How many solutions can I come up with? What is the best solution?"

3. Be aware of and avoid diversionary tactics. Your procrastination costs you big time. Make yourself aware of your "stall tactics" and call yourself on them. When you realize that you are spending time by wasting it, then restart.

4. Commitment begins with a decision. Decide to commit to your dreams today. Commitment is not only the gateway to success, but it will fill your life with purpose. It will give you a reason to awaken each day, provide energy, and fill you with enthusiasm.

5. Make a plan and implement it. What are your goals and dreams? Keep a journal to record them. Which one should you be working on first? What steps do you need to take to reach your goal? What are the dates that you will finish each step? Make a thorough plan and launch it.

6. Celebrate your success. Acknowledge your accomplishments and celebrate each one. Now that you've succeeded, you don't want to rest,

Rather, you want to maintain and sustain your successes; celebrating each one will encourage you to do so.

7. Rebound, Rebound, Rebound. Despite your successes, you may relapse and fall into a slump again. That is perfectly natural. So, expect future resistance and obstacles. Plan to smash through all barriers before they occur. Remind yourself that you are committed to success and will not allow anything to stand in your way.

8. Persist until you get it right and keep doing it right until it becomes a habit.

Personal Development Habits

1. Read 1 book per week. Reading is a good way to keep your brain active. With just 30 minutes per day you should be able to read one book per week, or more than 50 books per year.

2. Solve puzzles. Quizzes, word games, etc. are all good ways to exercise your brain.

Exit

3. Think positively. You are what you think all the time.

4. Make fast decisions. Instead of thinking for one hour wherever you are going to do something, make your decisions as fast as possible (usually less than 1 minute).

5. Meditate 30 minutes per day. A great way to gain clearness and peace is through meditation. 30 minutes are not a lot, but enough to get you started with meditation.

6. Have long- term goals and a plan of how to achieve them. Leaving nothing to chance.

7. The focus of short-term goals is an emphasis on completing daily actions.

8. Have a daily planner with the day's actions written down in order to keep track of what needs to be done, what has been done, and what was not accomplished.

9. Review each day at the end of the day to set tomorrow's actions and plan.

10. Value organization skills to avoid "clutter" in your life.

11. Update the way you work. Strive for efficiency and value driven activities.

12. Find a lesson, while others only see a problem.

13. Be solution focused.

14. Consciously and methodically create your own success, while others hope success will *find* them.

Attitude Habits

1. They are positive. Successful people don't let negative events alter their ego. They see the glass as half full. They boost the mood of others.

2. They take every opportunity they can. They are not afraid of doing something new, like giving a talk in public. They take everything as a challenge with themselves.

3. They use clear communication. There is a decision making process that can be explained to anyone. It is based on values and reasons, not excuses.

4. They do not complain. Everyone is able to complain about things. Bad things happen and complaining about them is not a good solution to stopping them from happening.

5. They offer their help for free. Successful people offer their help for free whenever they can. By giving you get, whether it is an internal feeling or an external/unexpected reward of some kind.

6. They smile. They smile often and genuinely.

7. Successful people are problem solvers. When something doesn't work as expected, they try to find solutions instead of complaining about the problem.

8. They over-deliver whenever possible.

9. They are genuinely interested in other people. Successful people are genuinely interested in building strong relationships with others.

10. They know how to listen. People like to talk. Why? Because they think there is someone listening, so in reality people like to be heard. Successful people talk less and listen more. If they don't know what to say, they ask questions instead of talking about themselves.

11. They make others feel important. Successful people stimulate ideas and conversations which lead to ideas.

12. Successful people can admit when they are wrong. If the blame sits with them, they take the responsibility.

13. They are encouraging and inspiring to others.

14. They are excited and motivated to deliver the best possible outcome with every opportunity.

15. Successful people are not afraid to fail, and often they expect a certain amount of failure. Failure is an integral part of learning, and successful people persist until they reach their goals.

16. They continue to learn and stay open-minded. They are constantly looking for new ways to increase efficiency and productivity. Seeking out ideas and information from multiple sources will bring you to a powerful conclusion.

17. They are persistent. Success does not happen overnight. It happens over many nights.

18. They are focused. Focus is an important element of productivity. Bringing projects to completion is also an important element of success.

19. They do not over extend themselves. This creates an unfocused and weak performing life. You must know what you can do, how you can do it, and when you can do it, just as you must know what you cannot do.

20. They are open minded. Everything changes. Successful people embrace changes and take advantage of technology to improve their business.

21. They are confident. Successful people believe in themselves and in their actions.

22. They start each day with positive input - from material that is listened to or read, helping them to remain positive throughout the day.

23. Successful people know that there is so much more yet to learn.

EMOTIONAL HABITS

1. They take time each day to be grateful for all of our gifts that are present in life.

2. They have a strong sense of self and know what they stand for.

3. They brush off criticism and do not dwell on the negative comments of others.

4. They attempt to remain calm and rational during hostile or chaotic situations.

5. They are fearful like everyone else, but they are not controlled by fear.

6. They are glass half full people – while still being practical and down-to-earth. They have an ability to *find the good in situations.*

7. They ask the right questions – the ones which put them in a productive, creative, positive mindset and emotional state.

8. They rarely complain (waste of energy). All complaining does is put the *complainer* in a negative and unproductive state.

9. They deal with problems and challenges quickly and effectively. They face their challenges and use them to improve themselves.

10. They don't believe in, or wait for fate, destiny, chance or luck to determine or shape their future. They believe in, and are committed to actively and consciously creating their own best life.

11. While many people are reactive, they are proactive. They take action before they *have* to.

12. They are more effective than most at managing their emotions. They feel like we all do but they are not slaves to their emotions.

Managing Your Own Anger
- Reframe self-talk
- Speak and listen nondefensively
- Deliberately calm yourself
- Find distractions

Managing Others' Anger
- Be asymmetrical; counteract rage with calm
- Validate the other person
- Probe
- Assume a problem orientation
- Refuse to be abused
- Disengage

13. They are good communicators and they consciously work at it.

14. They are humble and they are happy to admit mistakes and to apologize. They are confident in their ability, but not arrogant. They are happy to learn from others. They are happy to make others look good rather than seek their own personal glory.

15. They have identified their core values (what is important to them) and they do their best to live a life which is reflective of those values.

16. They understand the importance of discipline and self-control. They are strong. They are happy to take the road less travelled.

17. They are secure. They do not derive their sense of worth of self from what they own, who they know, where they live or what they look like.

18. They are generous and kind. They take pleasure in helping others achieve.

19. They understand the difference between control and controlling. They have their own opinion and allow others to have their own. Not everyone thinks alike. They allow for differences.

20. They live with a purpose - wake up each day knowing that they are working toward something great.

21. They maintain proper perspective.

22. They learn to live without regrets, and that life is the experiences that we choose.

Relationship Habits

1. Successful people don't criticize others; instead they seek alternate means from people and systems that will achieve the desired result.

2. They are calm, rational, and measured. Many successful people do not react to situations until they know how they want to react.

3. They are genuine. There are no facades with a truly successful person. They are clear, direct, and powerful. They are not weak willed or manipulative or forceful.

4. Love Unconditionally. Accept others for who they are. You don't put limitations on your love. Even though you may not always like the actions of your loved ones, – you continue to love them.

5. Choose Friends Wisely. Surround yourself with happy, positive people who share your values and goals. Friends that have the same ethics as you will encourage you to achieve your dreams. They help you to feel good about yourself. They are there to lend a helping hand when needed.

6. They are good communicators and they consciously work at it.

7. Successful people know how and when to compromise for the betterment of all parties in a relationship.

HEALTH HABITS

1. Always have a water bottle and drink from it often...water is the drink of choice, not soft drinks.

2. Look at exercise as a pleasure and privilege, not a burden or chore.

3. Think twice before deciding what to eat and why. Make sure that it is healthy(er) and will give your body good nutrition.

4. Measure intake based on your activity, not how you "feel". Need mandates intake, not mood.

5. Take action to solve problems when things get emotional, instead of turning to food as a cure.

6. Start the day with a well- balanced meal.

7. Drink a minimum amount of caffeine.

8. Always make time for relaxing and rewards at scheduled times.

9. See health as a privilege, not something to take for granted.

10. Contribute to the health of others by having a partner or friends to exercise with, as well as recruiting others who desire to get fit.

11. Learn new ways and new techniques for exercising.

12. Avoid monotony by taking up new forms of exercising.

13. Invest in workout clothes, good tennis shoes, and other apparel.

14. Never take your health for granted by taking a day off from a healthy life.

15. Know when too much of a good thing is no longer a good thing.

16. Respond to a challenge; do not react to what difficulties may be present.

17. Take a daily vitamin and mineral supplement that supports a healthy balance.

18. Make sure that you have adequate fiber sources in your diet for healthy human function.

19. Value good hygiene inside - the mind and organs and muscles - as well as on the outside - skin, hair, and nails.

20. Seek natural methods of health care - massage, exercise, physical therapy, naturopathic in addition to medical care.

21. Take exercise to new levels and challenge yourself.

22. Create a schedule for ultimate health and fitness.

23. Move beyond the boundaries of weight loss and into fitness.

24. Strive to reach your dreams every day and live each day to its fullest.

25. Avoid "wacky" diets and eating plans.

26. Get adequate amounts of sleep.

27. Avoid medications and drugs unless necessary.

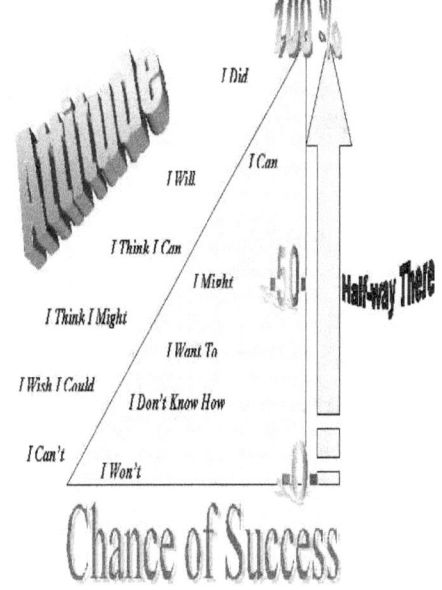

28. Limit alcohol intake only to special occasions.

29. Do what the average person does not want to do.

30. Exercise discipline by following a daily regimen.

31. Take a vacation by doing activities - jet skiing, snow skiing, mountain biking, hiking in the outback, golfing or going to a spa.

32. Know that life is fulfilling with optimal health in the mind, spirit and body!

Approach to life

1. Appreciate Life. Be thankful that you woke up alive each morning. Develop a childlike sense of wonder towards life. Focus on the beauty of every living thing. Make the most of each day. Don't take anything for granted. Don't sweat the small stuff.

2. Be Considerate. Accept others for who they are as well as where they are in life. Respect them for who they are. Touch them with a kind and generous spirit. Help when you are able, without trying to change the other person. Try to brighten the day of everyone you contact.

3. Learn Continuously. Keep up to date with the latest news regarding your career and hobbies. Try new and daring things that have sparked your interest – such as dancing, skiing, surfing or sky-diving.

4. Creative Problem Solving. Don't wallow in self-pity. As soon as you face a challenge get busy finding a solution. Don't let the setbacks affect your mood; instead see each new obstacle you face as an opportunity to make a positive change. Learn to trust your gut instinct – it's almost always right.

5. Do What You Love. Some statistics show that 80% of people dislike their jobs! No wonder there's so many unhappy people running around. We spend a great deal of our life working. Choose a career that you enjoy – the extra money of a job you detest isn't worth it. Make time to enjoy your hobbies and pursue special interests.

6. Have fun. Take the time to see the beauty around you. There's more to life than work. Take time to smell the roses, watch a sunset or sunrise with a loved one, take a walk along the seashore, hike in the woods etc. Learn to live in the present moment and cherish it. Don't live in the past or the future.

7. Laugh. Don't take yourself – or life too seriously. You can find humor in just about any situation. Laugh at yourself – no one's perfect. When appropriate laugh and make light of the circumstances. (Naturally there are times that you should be serious as it would be improper to laugh.)

8. Forgive. Holding a grudge will hurt no one but you. Forgive others for your own peace of mind. When you make a mistake – own up to it – learn from it – and FORGIVE yourself.

9. Gratitude. Develop an attitude of gratitude. Count all your blessings - even the things that seem trivial. Be grateful for your home, your work and most importantly your family and friends. Take the time to tell them that you are happy they are in your life.

10. Invest in Relationships. Always make sure your loved ones know you love them even in times of conflict. Nurture and grow your relationships with your family and friends by making the time to spend with them. Don't break your promises to them. Be supportive.

11. Keep Your Word. Honesty is the best policy. Every action and decision you make should be based on honesty. Be honest with yourself and with your loved ones.

12. Mind Your Own Business. Concentrate on creating your life the way you want it. Take care of you and your family. Don't get overly concerned with what other people are doing or saying. Don't get caught up with gossip or name calling. Don't judge. Everyone has a right to live their own life the way they want to – including you.

13. Optimism. See the glass as half full. Find the positive side of any given situation. It's there – even though it may be hard to find. Know that everything happens for a reason, even though you may never know what the reason is. Steer clear of negative thoughts. If a negative thought creeps in, – replace it with a positive thought.

14. Persistence. Never give up. Face each new challenge with the attitude that it will bring you one step closer to your goal. You will never fail, as long as you never give up. Focus on what you want, learn the required skills, make a plan to succeed, and take action. We are always happiest while pursuing something of value to us.

15. Be Proactive. Accept what cannot be changed. Happy people don't waste energy on circumstances beyond their control. Accept your limitations as a human being. Determine how you can take control by creating the outcome you desire, rather than waiting to respond.

16. Self Care. Take care of your mind, body and health. Get regular medical check- ups. Eat healthy and work out. Get plenty of rest. Drink lots of water. Exercise your mind by continually energizing it with interesting and exciting challenges.

17. Self Confidence. Don't try to be someone that you're not. After all no one likes a phony. Determine who you are in the inside – your own personal likes and dislikes. Be confident in who you are. Do the best you can and don't second guess yourself.

18. Take Responsibility. Happy people know and understand that they are 100% responsible for their life. They take responsibility for their moods, attitude, thoughts, feelings, actions and words. They are the first to admit when they've made a mistake.

Begin today by taking responsibility for your happiness. Work on developing these habits as you own. The more you incorporate the above habits into your daily lifestyle – the happier you will be.

Most of all: BE TRUE TO YOURSELF.

Lifestyle Habits

1. Live a balanced life - exercise, work, family, and a Higher Power.

2. They look for and find opportunities where others see nothing.

3. They take complete responsibility for their actions and outcomes (or lack thereof).

4. While they are not necessarily more talented than the majority, they always find a way to maximize their potential. They get more out of themselves. They use what they have more effectively.

5. They are busy, productive and proactive. While most are lying on the couch, planning, over-thinking, sitting on their hands and generally going around in circles, they are out there getting the job done.

6. They align themselves with like-minded people. They understand the importance of being part of a team. They create win-win relationships.

7. They are ambitious. They consciously choose to live their best life rather than spending it on auto-pilot.

8. They have clarity and certainty about what they want (and don't want) for their life.

9. They don't procrastinate and they don't spend their life waiting for the "right time".

10. They are life-long learners. They constantly work at educating themselves, either formally (academically), informally (watching, listening, asking, reading, student of life) or experientially (doing, trying)… or all three.

11. They consistently do what they need to do, regardless of how they are *feeling* on a given day. They don't spend their life stopping and starting.

12. They take calculated risks – financial, emotional, professional, and psychological.

13. They become exceptional by choice. We're all faced with life-shaping decisions daily. Successful people make the decisions that most won't and don't.

14. While many people are pleasure junkies and avoid pain and discomfort at all costs, successful people understand the value and benefits of working through the tough stuff that most would avoid.

15. They are adaptable and embrace change, while the majority is creatures of comfort and habit. They are comfortable with, and embrace, the new and the unfamiliar.

16. They keep themselves in shape physically. They understand the importance of being physically well. They are not all about looks; they are more concerned with function and health. Their body is not *who they are*, it's where they live.

17. They are open to, and more likely to act upon, feedback.

18. They are careful to select their friends and influences.

19. They don't invest time or emotional energy into things where they have no control.

20. They are not *people pleasers* and they don't need constant approval.

21. They are more comfortable with their own company than most.

22. They set higher standards for themselves which in turn produces greater commitment, more momentum, and a better work ethic and of course, better results.

23. They don't rationalize failure. While many are talking about their age, their sore back, their lack of time, their poor genetics, their 'bad luck', their nasty boss and their lack of opportunities (all good *reasons* to fail), they are finding a way to succeed *despite* all their challenges.

24. They have an *off switch*. They know how to relax, enjoy what they have in their life and to have fun.

25. They are more interested in *effective* than they are in *easy*. While the majority look for the quickest, easiest way (the shortcut), they look for the course of action which will produce the best results over the long term.

26. They finish what they start. While so many spend their life starting things that they never finish, successful people get the job done – even when the excitement and the novelty have worn off. Even when it isn't *fun*.

27. They are multi-dimensional, complex creatures. They realize that not only are they physical and psychological beings, but emotional and spiritual creatures as well. They consciously work at being *healthy* and productive on all levels.

28. They practice what they preach. They don't talk about the theory, they live the reality.

Financial Habits

1. They have balance. While they *may* be financially successful, they know that the terms *money* and *success* are not interchangeable. They understand that people, who are successful on a financial level only, are not successful at all. Unfortunately we live in a society which teaches that money equals success. Like many other things, money is a tool. It's certainly not a bad thing but ultimately, it's just another resource. Unfortunately, too many people worship it.

2. Wait 48 hours before buying anything to eliminate impulse purchases and buyer's remorse. It is a tremendous money saver, try it.

3. They have a plan for their life and they work methodically at turning that plan into a reality. Their life is not a clumsy series of unplanned events and outcomes.

4. Their career is not their identity, it's their job. It's not who they are, it's what they do.

5. They save for their future. A minimum of 10% (20% is ideal)of Gross Earnings should go your retirement accounts.

Habits that derail success

1. You Procrastinate. You keep putting things off. You talk about how you want to do something but you don't act on it. Why? Because it's not painful enough. You procrastinate on taking action because the situation is not painful enough for you yet.

2. You underestimate your goal. Achieving a goal is about getting from point A to B. Almost all the time, people fail because they underestimate what it takes to achieve their goals. Adjust your plan of action and adapt accordingly.

3. You spend more time defending your problems than taking action. You complain how you are not getting XYZ results. When people try to give you suggestions, you spend more time justifying why their suggestions will not work and defending your lack of results than brainstorming with them on how to get out of your rut. Spend less time talking about your problems and use that time to think about solutions. Then act on them. You'll get a lot more results this way, and you'll be happier.

4. You're too enclosed in your own world. You don't venture out beyond your normal routine. You do the same things, talk to the same old friends, act the same way. Open yourself up – take active steps to grow. Get to know more people – people who are driven, positive and focused. Get new, refreshing perspectives.

5. You are fearful. (Avoidance (Fear)). You avoid taking action because some of the things you have to do intimidate you. You rather delay the process as much as possible. Face the fear and do it anyway.

6. You get easily distracted. You get distracted by things thrown in your way. Your attention gets diverted from your goals. Your ability to stay focused is instrumental to achieving your results. Be clear in what you want and stick to it. Don't let anything (or anyone) distract you.

7. You over-complicate situations. Common among the neurotic perfectionists. If you are a neurotic perfectionist, you blow the situation out of proportion and create this mental image that's so complicated that it's no wonder you don't get anything done. Things are usually simpler than you think – be conscious when you are adding unnecessary complications for yourself.

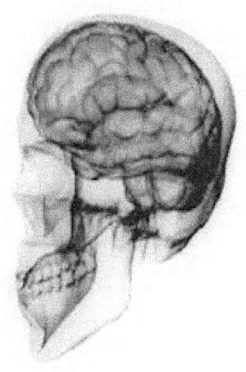

Your Mind has

Total Control

over Your Actions

8. You have made a habit out of quitting. You give up before you even get anywhere.

9. You lose sight of your goals. You settle for less, forgetting the goals you once set. You have to first reconnect with your inner desires. What is the future you want to create for yourself? Reignite your vision and don't ever lose sight of it.

10. You are closed minded and ignorant. You insist on doing things a certain way. You don't open yourself up to new ideas. Open yourself to new methods. Experiment. You can only improve if you are willing to try new things.

TRANSFORM · YOUR THINKING · YOUR BODY · YOUR LIFE

It is Time to FOCUS

What is holding you back?
Choose 2-3 challenges to focus on and overcome this week.

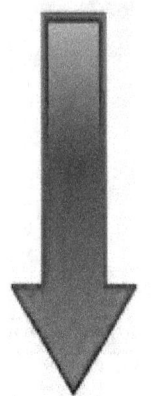

↓ Wine/Beer and/or WHine
↓ Desserts and reactive eating
↓ Justifications
↓ Tired
↓ Limiting Beliefs/ Negative Self-talk
↓ Wasting Time
↓ Feeling bad
↓ Being unprepared
↓ Accepting where you are
↓ Emotional Eating
↓ Sitting
↓ Wishing things would change

↑ Breakfast
↑ Water/ Hydration
↑ Movement
↑ Focus on Realistic/Positive Thinking
↑ Planning
↑ Expectations for YOUR life
↑ Self Worth/ Value
↑ Productivity
↑ Powerful internal talk during Exercise
↑ Meal Frequency and Consistency
↑ Fuel Feeding
↑ Thinking and Reading (20/20/20)
↑ Surprise Exercise
↑ Fruit and Veggie Intake
↑ ACTION

ELIMINATE THIS WORD!

Get Motivated – Get Educated
Take Control – Get Results
www.InnovationFitness.net

CHAPTER 4

DEEP THINKERS - SELF COACHING 101

**"If you want to know your past -- look into your present conditions.
If you want to know your future -- look into your present actions."
-Chinese Proverb**

In this section:

- Create your long term Vision
- Determine your Values and Priorities
- Become aware of your "landmines".
- Create short and long term goals.
- Begin to put together your plan for success.

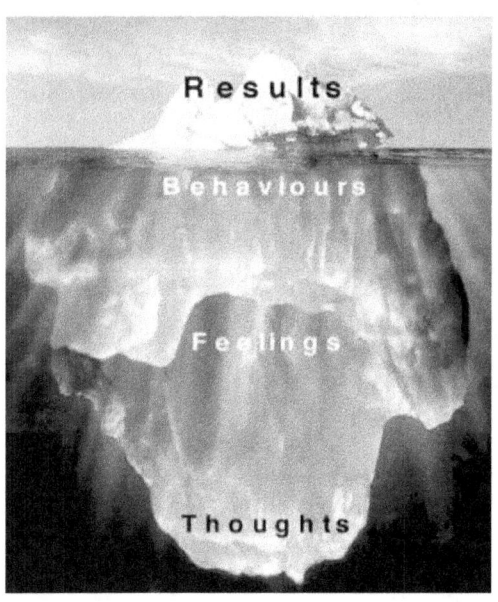

DECIDE
TAKE ACTION
GET RESULTS!

Key to success:

No matter how you define fitness—whether it's a desired physical appearance or an overall feeling—make your definition clear, concise, and achievable. This will help you in developing your fitness goals.

Direction - Goals direct action. They channel and focus effort in the direction chosen by you. As a result, they are empowering tools, enabling you to steer your life in the direction of your choosing.

Motivation - Goals stretch and push, resulting in greater effort and persistence. Goals clarify and make concrete your desired ends. Being aware of the gap between where you are now and where you want to be creates motivation to close that gap.

Strategy refinement - After setting challenging goals, people think longer and more creatively about how to accomplish them and how to measure progress toward them.

-Dr. Steven Krauss PHD

SELF COACHING

"For true success ask yourself these four questions: Why? Why not? Why not me? Why not now?" - James Allen

Remember this equation:

- + - = -   A negative plus a negative has only one outcome.
- + + = ?   A negative plus a positive has multiple outcomes.
+ + + = +   This is ideal. Be positive and surround yourself with positive support.

Why do we resist change?
Change represents giving up part of our old selves and allowing something unknown/new to emerge.

Creating a healthy lifestyle does not happen by accident. To reach and maintain your goals, you need to have a plan.

People who achieve nothing are, in reality, achieving what they think they deserve: nothing.
Expect more from yourself, get more for yourself.

Continually ask yourself the following questions:
- What exactly am I trying to achieve?

- What is the exact strategy I am using to achieve it?

- In what areas am I producing the results I desire?

- In what areas am I not producing optimal results?

- Which part of my process is not performing?

- How can I adapt that part of the process so I can test my modified strategy against the desired result?

- What would happen if I completely reinvented my strategy?

- Most important: What can I do right now to help me achieve my goal?

MEASURING YOUR FITNESS LIFESTYLE
Are You Ready to Make a Lifestyle Change?

What's Your Lifestyle Like?
The reason lifestyle is so important is because how you live determines your choices and these choices decide how healthy you are and whether you're on the road to weight loss. So what is a healthy lifestyle? The typical components include not smoking, eating healthy foods, exercising and keeping the body at a healthy weight. Where do you fall on the healthy lifestyle continuum?

First, figure out how much time you spend doing the following:

Hours per Day	Hours Per Week	
		Sitting at a desk
		Sitting in a car
		Sitting in front of a TV
		Sitting in front of a computer
		Eating out at restaurants
		Drinking alcohol
		Eating fast food or junk foods
		Staying up late/not getting enough sleep

Now, how much time do you spend?

Hours per Day	Hours Per Week	
		Being active in general
		Doing cardio exercise
		Strength training with challenging weights
		Preparing your own healthy meals and snacks
		Reading food labels
		Tracking your calories
		Sleeping
		Dealing with stress in a healthy way

If you spend more time doing the things in the first list than the second, it's time to reevaluate your priorities and decide what you really want for yourself. Living healthy means spending time and energy on your body--moving it around and paying attention to what you put into it. Staying in an unhealthy lifestyle means you can avoid expending energy, time and effort...but at what cost?

The rewards for making these changes are endless, but it's beginning that's so difficult.

Choosing Health and Fitness for High Performance Living

As humans, we like habits and routines, so much that we often keep doing the same things even when we know they aren't good for us. Changing bad habits takes time and effort and, for a healthy lifestyle, you may be changing a variety of things like:

Current:	New Habit:

What time you get up each morning?

What time you go to bed each night?

How you spend your free time?

How you spend your money?

How you shop, cook and eat?

How much TV you watch?

What you do with your family and friends?

How much time do you spend planning your week?

Goal Setting 101

What do you want?
List your goals then prioritize them.

Now make them more specific:

Plan: What will you do to achieve them?

Schedule: How will you execute your plan?
Daily, Weekly, Monthly, Annually etc...

Measure: How will you measure your success?

What course/habit changes will you alter to change your present circumstance/ result?

Obstacles: What would prevent you from achieving your goals?

What is your setback plan?

SMART Goals

S = Specific

M = Measurable

A = Achievable

R = Relevant

T = Time-Bound

CREATING YOUR VISION

---

5 Steps to creating a Powerful Vision:

1. State your outcome. What do you want to achieve in positive terms.
2. Specificity. Close your eyes, how does your outcome look, what do you feel like, and what does it sound like, smell like?   Utilize all of your senses to move closer to your vision.
3. Have measurable results. What will you look like, how will you feel, how will the external world see and hear you.

VISION: Who do I want to be?

<u>Attributes and Attitudes</u>
1.
2.
3.
4.
5.

POWERFUL QUESTIONS TO AID YOU IN CREATING YOUR VISION

1. What is my personal definition of success?

2. What am I passionate about? What lights me up and brings me joy?

3. What are my special gifts and talents and how am I using them every day?

4. Does my work currently bring me meaning and fulfillment and allow me to express my uniqueness?

5. What do I often dream about doing that I have never done?

6. What is my **BIG** vision of what's possible for the world? How can I make a difference?

7. Which three personal qualities do I value most, and how deeply am I expressing them in my relationships and in my work? (Examples: truthfulness, love, spontaneity, fun, leadership, inclusiveness, mastery, positive attitude, presence, joy, creativity, peacefulness, committed)

Once you have your answers to these questions, ask yourself what actions you could take to make these changes and to give your gifts and talents fully to your work and to the world. Most often, it's the smaller steps we take on a consistent basis that bring about renewal, rather than major changes.

Vision Statement:
Once you remove your limiting beliefs you can fill your life with possibilities and the education needed to make change last.

3V – YOUR VALUES AND PRIORITIES
Identify your Core Values and Priorities

The first step to success is figuring out what you stand for and ultimately what you will absolutely not stand for. Core values will define the way in which you think, act, and judge the results you received. In an ever-changing world your core values remain the constant. Your ability to commit to your values in the face of adversity defines you as a person. Values will guide you and motivate you. If you have not done the work to identify your core values there is no better time than now. In table 1 you will find a list of values, begin by circling ten values, then take that list and begin to prioritize that list until you can narrow down to three to five core values.

1 - Personal Values - Example Beliefs	Values	Behaviors
1. If you do not lie to yourself you have infinite power	Honesty	Always speak from the heart
2. In life a strong foundation is needed	Family	Spend time w/family
3. Live life in the 10 inches in front of you	Passion	Enjoy what I have in present
4. Trust that someone is watching you from above	Faith	Pray, believe & trust in one

Table 1

1. Accountability

2. Achievement

3. Adaptability

4. Balance

5. Being the best

6. Blame

7. Caring for others

8. Challenge

9. Clear precise goals

10. Wisdom

11. Coaching

12. Collaboration

13. Commitment

14. Community

15. Compassion

16. Competence

17. Control

18. Cooperation

19. Vision

20. Creativity

21. Diversity

22. Efficiency

23. Trust

24. Empowerment

25. Enthusiasm

26. Entrepreneurship

27. Environment

28. Ethics

29. Family

30. Financial stability

31. Friendship

32. Generosity

33. Honesty

34. Humor

35. Independence

36. Innovation

37. Integrity

38. Job security

39. Knowledge

40. Leadership

41. Learning

42. Long term planning

43. Loyalty

44. Openness

45. Passion

46. Personal Growth

47. Power

48. Productivity

49. Professionalism

50. Profit

51. Quality

52. Respect

53. Risk-taking

54. Service

55. Spirituality

56. Teamwork

57. Tradition

It is important to remember that you can have different values for the different roles in your life. The most obvious is your personal and professional values. Here is an example of a Personal Value Sheet.

My Beliefs:	My values:	My Behaviors:
1.		
2.		
3.		
4.		

Once you establish your vision begin to look at the similarities between your values and your vision. This is where absolute decision making comes from.

Live to your values, vision and virtues (3V).

AWARENESS
Here is a tool to aid you in staying present and focused to your environment and goals

The point of mindfulness is not to judge our thoughts, but to simply observe them more closely. From that awareness we can ask open questions to deepen our understanding while decreasing the space between what we want and what is happening inside of us. When we are experiencing a particularly powerful state of mind, we can stop and ask:

- What exactly am I feeling?

- What is happening in my mind at this present moment?

- Is this pattern of thought useful?

- If not, what thought would be?

- If that thought were the predominant one in my mind, in what ways would that affect my behavior?

- What one action can I take now that is in correspondence with that thought?

Because of our drive for consistency, we can change our state of mind by being keenly aware of what we are thinking, and, when appropriate, changing what we are doing. As a result, we are prone to rationalize our change in behavior and ensuing thought, reinforcing it as a more permanent pattern.

1) **What will I do today, tomorrow, next week, next month to cause my goal(s) to happen?**
   Self initiated and self controlled actions.

   What R.P.M. changes can be done now?

   Next week?

2) **Why do you feel prepared to start now?**
   Why do you believe in yourself?

   Why are you worth this?

3) Do I have everything I need (physical, mental, emotional) to achieve my goal?

Do you have all the resources necessary to be successful?

If no, what do you feel you need in order to be successful?

4) What else would change?

What would stay the same?

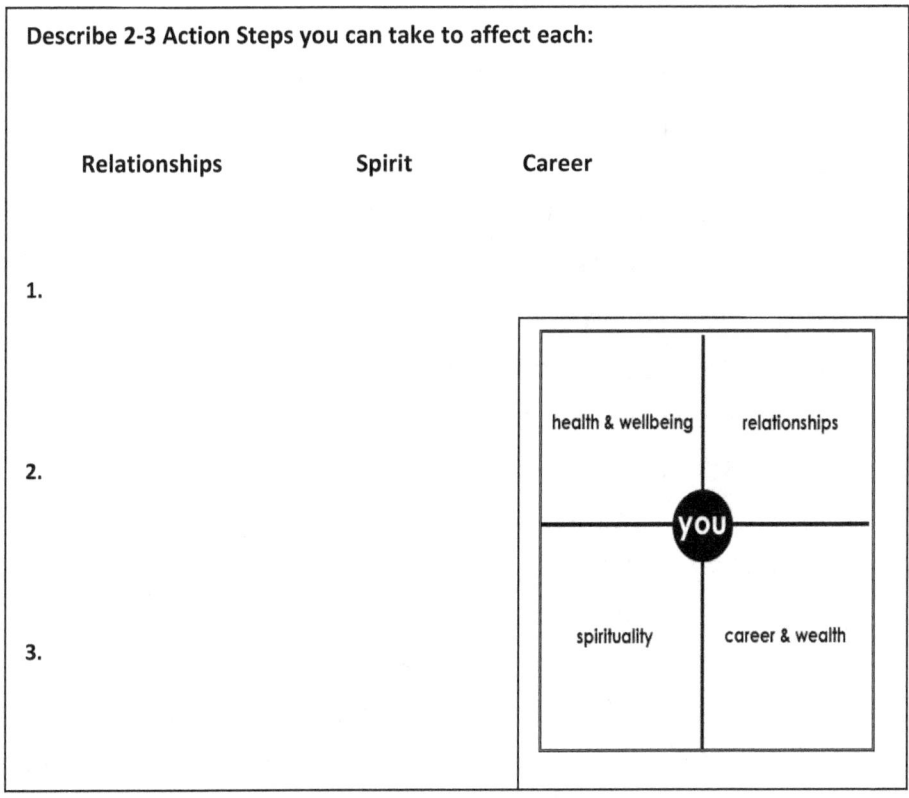

Describe 2-3 Action Steps you can take to affect each:

	Relationships	Spirit	Career
1.			
2.			
3.			

Your Formula for Daily Success:

Read this daily for continued **inspiration**.

- ✓ Accept No Limits
- ✓ Conquer Doubt
- ✓ Put Off Procrastination
- ✓ Don't Quit
- ✓ Live In the Solution
- ✓ Take Responsibility
- ✓ See Yourself Succeed
- ✓ Focus On Ideas
- ✓ Every Circumstance Has Two Sides
- ✓ Master Your Fears
- ✓ Persist
- ✓ Directed Thoughts
- ✓ Be Blind To Failure
- ✓ Decide To Grow
- ✓ Create Your Own Circumstance
- ✓ Problems Bring Lessons
- ✓ Persistence
- ✓ Identify Your Vision
- ✓ Thoughts Create your Behavior
- ✓ Control Your Destiny
- ✓ Expect to lose weight over time
- ✓ Focus on both Long Term and Short Term Goals
- ✓ Find out how many calories are in your favorite foods
- ✓ Commit to the commitment.
- ✓ Strive for consistency
- ✓ Your habits determine your outcome

Your List of Daily Questions:

Utilize MINDFUL choices over MINDLESS ones for long-term success.

- ✓ Did I Eat Breakfast?
- ✓ Did I Take My Multi Vitamin?
- ✓ Did I Journal?
- ✓ Did I Find Ways to Add In 'Surprise exercise'?
- ✓ Did I Stay Positive?
- ✓ Did I find 10- Minutes to Be with My Thoughts?
- ✓ How Have I Helped Myself?
- ✓ How many times did I eat today?
- ✓ Did I eat balanced meals (P,C,F)?
- ✓ Did I eat every 3–4 hours, not going more than 5 hours without eating?
- ✓ How much time did I spend reading today?
- ✓ What were my reasons to smile today?
- ✓ When was I the most alert and energetic?
- ✓ How do you think your energy affected what you ate?
- ✓ How do you think what you ate affected your energy?
- ✓ How do you think your thoughts affected your energy?
- ✓ What was my BIGGEST Challenge today?
- ✓ How did I resolve it?

MAKE A LIST OF "MUST DO'S" FOR THE DAY TO BE A SUCCESS

Monday	Tuesday	Wednesday	Thursday	Friday	Saturday

✕TRANSFORM · YOUR THINKING · YOUR BODY · YOUR LIFE

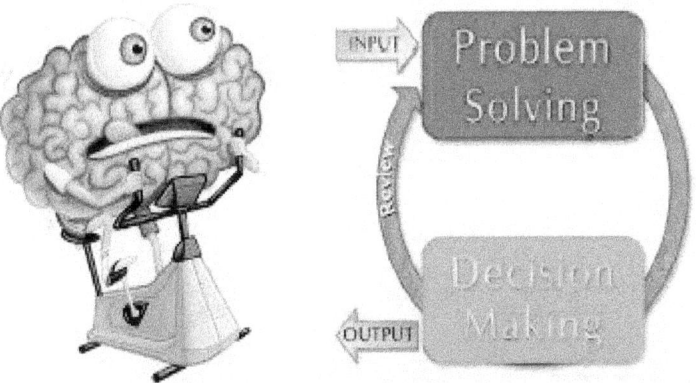

The 4 questions for change
www.InnovationFitness.net

What are the advantages of changing?	What are the disadvantages of changing?	What are the advantages of NOT changing?	What are the disadvantages of NOT changing?

The 4 methods of change
www.InnovationFitness.net

START a completely new action	**STOP** doing something entirely	Do **MORE** of something	Do **LESS** of something

The 3 questions for Action
www.InnovationFitness.net

What Actions **can I** take?	What **can I** read?	Who **can I** ask?

Get Motivated – Get Educated
Take Control – Get Results
www.InnovationFitness.net

CHAPTER 5

THE SUCCESS RULES

Creating lasting change is rewarding. It is also filled with obstacles that must be solved. Success is just around the corner. YOU are worth it.

A review of the content delivered in a fun way.
This will be your reference tool.

Knowledge is ~~Power~~ Potential
Execution = Success
Often, the difference between success and failure is execution.
I believe that most of us have more than enough
knowledge and information to make changes in our
health, fitness, careers and relationships. We do not
lack direction. We lack focus and action. Action =
Success.
The most vital ingredient to success is continued
action.

KNOWLEDGE IS POWER

We know healthy from unhealthy, and we know
movement is better than sitting on the couch. We
know patience is better than impatience, and we
know that communication is better than shutting
down. That is enough to begin. Change begins with
the choice for action.

Do what needs to be done.
What Action Steps can you take to improve your:
Health:
Fitness:
Finances:
Relationships:

Change is inevitable. Growth is optional.

Few things in life are certain.
Change is one of them. Learning
to embrace change is a powerful
tool to allow continued growth
and success.

Choosing the opposite stance will
simply keep you where you are
while the world continues ahead.

Do you want Personal Growth?
Then embrace change.

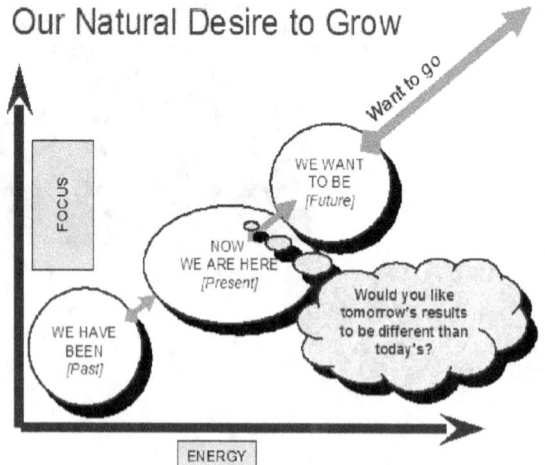

Our Natural Desire to Grow

Want to go

FOCUS

WE WANT
TO BE
[Future]

NOW
WE ARE HERE
[Present]

Would you like
tomorrow's results
to be different than
today's?

WE HAVE
BEEN
[Past]

ENERGY

92

How can you achieve something if you don't know what it is?

Goal setting is a simple yet overlooked exercise. People who have goals achieve more than others that do not.

Do you have goals? Are they clear and specific? Do you know WHY you have set your goals?

If your goals are not clear and concrete, then you should not be surprised if you do not get what you want.

Clear goals = Clear Outcomes.

Make your actions count towards your goals.

Often, people are at odds with themselves. They desire achievement but do not act out the steps necessary to make the changes. Measure your impact, not your intentions. Set your goals, work your plan and get your results or don't.

If you are not achieving the desired results then your plan **does not** work. Go back to Goal Setting, gain the necessary clarity to move forward and then set your Action Plan. Remember, Goals are WHAT's. Action Steps are the HOW's of Goal Achievement.

Same = Same, Change = Change

If you do the same thing, you will get the same result. If you create new,

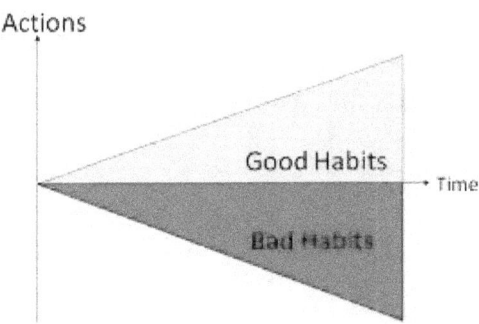

worse habits your results will prove to be worse over time. Perhaps not immediately, but they will eventually catch up to you.

If you create new, better habits then results will improve slowly at first and faster as they compound.

Commit to identifying your Helping Habits and Hurting Habits. Modify them as necessary. DO NOT go through life mindlessly.

One step at a time.

Your plan of action should be staged to accomplish one thing at a time. Avoid the **"all or none"** mindset of not acting then trying to do everything at once. Or trying to achieve "Perfection" but getting discouraged when you realize that you cannot accomplish everything you FELT that you could.

Set goals that you know you will achieve, build momentum from there and then layer more goals atop your new, current actions. You will be amazed at how much gets accomplished in this fashion vs. the continual start and stop cycle that most people employ.

A -> B. Then B -> C.

Change Bank Theory: Everything is Cumulative

Have you ever saved your pocket change? You begin with an empty container and slowly empty your pockets daily until the container is full. At first, you do not have much at all, a few quarters, a handful of pennies, and a couple of nickels and dimes… However, over time, a few weeks or months the change begins to accumulate and add up. After a year or so, you may have even saved a few hundred dollars. This is the philosophy to take with you. We are creating ways to increase positive outcomes.

Find ways to save quarters (big changes/habits) and dimes, nickels and pennies (small changes/habits) in your daily life. It all adds up.

How can you employ "Change Bank" to –

Health:

Fitness:

Finances:

Relationships:

Get into the process and out of the outcome.

An important point to understand is that results/success does not happen immediately. If you are focused on the goals rather than what you are doing to attain the goal then you will be disappointed in the pace and may even give up (like most do).

Own the process, do the work and the results will happen in time.

Life never happens in a straight arrow. There are

Maintenance
(works to sustain the behavior change)

Action
(practices the desired behavior)

Preparation
(intends to take action)

Contemplation
(aware of the problem and of the desired behavior change)

Precontemplation
(unaware of the problem)

The Stages of Behavior Change

Sources: Grimley 1997 (75) and Prochaska 1992 (148)

many turns, setbacks, detours, diversions and changes. Stay focused on the goals and the actions needed to attain your successes.

Stay Positive, Plan Ahead and Learn to Rebound from Setbacks.

A staple philosophy. Being negative is futile. So stay positive. It can only help.

Plan ahead for meals, to do lists, finances and other priorities. Planning means you are prepared. A lack of planning means that you are unprepared.

Rebound from setbacks simply means that no matter what your plans are there will be changes to circumstances that are out of your control. PLAN for the unplanned by knowing that the unknown is coming and you will be able to adapt and continue your progress.

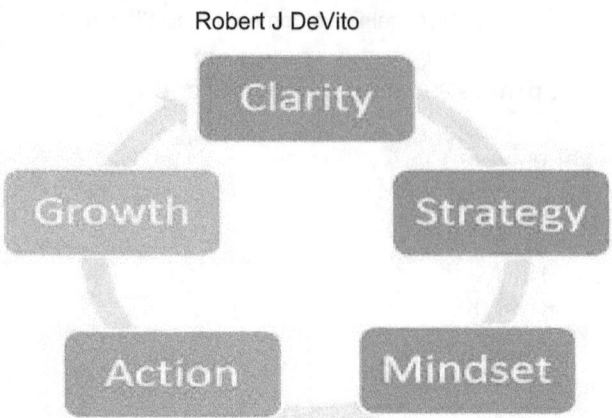

Be Present.

If you find yourself continually thinking of things other than what you are doing then it is time for a reset. Do what you are doing when you are doing it. Your focus and production will increase dramatically.

Monitor your self-talk and your thoughts. Are you drifting form the task at hand? Are you singularly focused to a completion? Are you giving your best in the current situation?

work   home

Your Habits have a Cost.

Consider the cost (Positive and Negative) to your habits. Every action you take has a cost. Are your actions worth the costs and efforts of doing them? Gain the needed clarity of your actions by measuring the action, the effort and the ultimate cost to your life.

Critical Thinking or Thinking "Critically"

I have found that most of the successful people that I know are critical thinkers, while most of the people that consistently struggle for success think critically of themselves, others and circumstances.

Critical thinking is using your Knowledge, Experience and Common Sense to create a SOLUTION for challenges and obstacles. Thinking Critically is the opposite. The type of person that consistently finds the challenge in the challenge and always seems to find him or herself embroiled in controversy at home, with friends or at work is Thinking Critically. They have trained themselves to find the worst in people and situations. Chances are high that this person spends a great deal of time trying to convince people that their way is best and that everyone else is either bad or wrong. <u>You cannot be focused on the issue and the solution simultaneously.</u>

Begin to notice when you are Thinking Critically and then apply critical thinking to the situation. Discover your patterns and obstacles and break them. Critical Thinking delivers solutions from a logical standpoint. Critical Thinking allows you to view a situation of its own accord, without interference from past feelings or biases. *Critical Thinking is Solution Based Thinking.*

Clear thinking = Good Outcomes.

Update How You Work

Constantly be in search of ways to improve your efficiency. Time Effectiveness tools are available everywhere. Perhaps it is pulling out the Daily To Do List or switching to a planner in your Smartphone or syncing your communication devices and schedules. Whatever needs to be done to improve efficiency and effectiveness should be done NOW.

Don't fall victim to B.S.

If you have ever watched television at 3AM you know
that you can lose 30 lbs in a month, get rock hard "abs",
get filthy rich selling houses or trading stocks, improve
your IQ and health by swallowing a scientifically amazing
dietary supplement AND find the partner of your dreams
(All for just two payments of $39.95 each…).

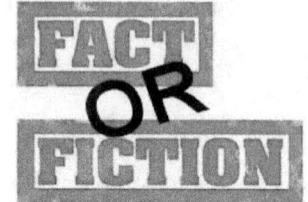

These false promises and hyperbole are effective because they prey on sleep
deprived, emotionally drained and desperate people. We all are at this point
sometimes. Life can take its toll on you of you let it. However, *logic has to
prove out over emotion* and you must be intelligent and patient enough to know
not to fall victim to these ridiculous claims and scams. Intelligent work
applied consistently over time will bring the best long-term results.

Balance Creates Balance

In an ideal world, our lives would mirror this
scenario: All of the facets of life and its' demands
would be evenly distributed and manageable. We
would live relatively stress free and find simple,
quick solutions to our issues. This rarely, if ever
happens and usually we can point to one or two
areas that are creating more stress than others are.

This is either due to something unavoidable, as our unpredictable life is
destined to do periodically, or, something that we, ourselves create.

Regardless of the reason, we will benefit greatly from remaining aware of our
life balance and striving to not be pulled too hard for too long in any one
direction. Allowing ourselves to put the focus where it is needed at the time
it is needed will reduce overall stress and increase long-term success. You will
need to devote attention to the "must dos" of life. There is no way around
this. However, insuring that you create some balance in life no matter the
circumstance(s) by taking care of yourself physically and mentally is of
paramount importance.

Not everything is urgent and important all of the time. Put the task in its'
proper place.

Doubt Doubt.

If you constantly doubt yourself, just consider how futile your pessimistic attitude is. If you do not stand for you AND believe in you then why would anyone else? Replace feelings of doubt with conscious choices and actions. The chances are that doubting yourself has not gotten you your desired outcome. Now seems like a great time to alter that thought pattern.

The way to overcome doubt is with ACTION.

A simple exercise to create confidence is to make a list of the times that you doubted yourself and then list the outcome. Most likely, the outcome was much better and stronger than you envisioned. Store this in your "Confidence Column". You have accomplished many more things much easier than you give yourself the credit for. Begin to not only "Believe" it, but know it from the facts.

Banish Can't – You Can if You Choose to

I would love to have the word "Can't" removed from the dictionary. I have seen so many people tell themselves and anyone else that will listen that they cannot do something even before they have tried. You simply need to want something for yourself more than you do not want something else. You can. It takes perseverance and desire to overcome doubt and fear. You can do it. Everything is a process and nothing but decisions happen instantaneously. Just choose success.

Live your life so you can feel the positive emotions much more than the negative emotions. Your thoughts about yourself and others and hence, your action will determine which list you spend most of your time in. Break the cycle of negativity.

Feel Your Feelings

Become aware of how you are feeling at a given moment. Become adept at understanding why you are feeling the way you are. When you can get to the root cause of your feelings and understand the motivation of your feelings and actions you will have the power to change them.

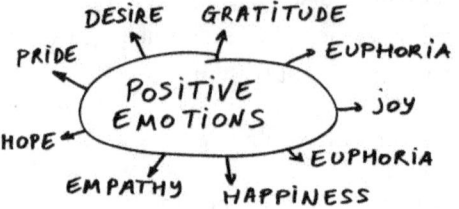
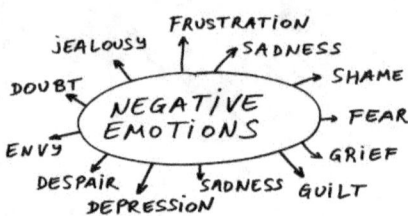

Energy is a Choice

Stop Being Tired

Many of us will not have enough sleep; we will always want to reach for the "snooze button" repeatedly, we will feel fatigued throughout the day and feel as though we are never rested and energetic. All of this may actually be true.

You may never get the rest and relaxation you desire. You may be fatigued (especially if you do not exercise regularly and fuel your body properly) and you may have a "to-do" list that is ½ mile long. Choose Energy.

If you are used to telling yourself that you are tired then you will be tired. You are not more tired or busier than anyone else is. We are all busy and tired and have the "to do" list. Some people get things done and other do not. Work ethic accounts for a percentage but so does will. Choose Energy. Tell yourself that you are not tired instead of telling yourself how tired you are. It is your choice.

Taking Care of Yourself

Good Nutrition Pays

Treat your body right and create a high performance machine by consistently feeding your body healthy and nutritious foods.

Love Exercise

Get the most from your machine by keeping yourself in good physical shape. Take part in multiple types of fitness and exercise. Get outside and try new things, go for a walk with your family to reenergize and make a commitment to movement every day. You will have more energy to take on more and do more.

Mental Fitness

Continue your development by acquiring new skills. Read daily, gain insight from mentors and coaches and fill your downtime with educational materials.

Honesty Covenant

Having an *Honesty Covenant* with yourself and others will be essential to your success and mental well-being. In reality, the scale/checkbook/relationships/happiness does not lie. Misleading yourself or others as to how well you are behaving but just not seeing the results is  detrimental to success. Beyond being in a Physiological Plateau, here are the reasons I see that people do not succeed:

- You were not ready to commit to a new/different lifestyle.
- You did not know how to get started, and stay on the right track.
- You lacked the proper information/education.
- You wanted a quick fix.

Be honest with yourself and others. Ask for help when you need to and stay the course.

Figure out what issues/challenges you face and find long-term solutions. If you are not changing, then there is an issue with one of the following:

Food - Fitness – Focus

Have you been honest?

If not, how have you been deceiving yourself?

How can you course correct?

Do the Next Right Thing. That is all you can do anyway.

Superheroes are fictional characters. They fight evil and always do the right thing. In reality, we are human beings and that means we are fallible and will make many mistakes in every single facet of life. When it comes to weight loss, we will all take steps backwards. Our choices will lead to a stop in weight loss or even a bit of weight gain from time to time. It will happen, prepare for it. Our choices will lead us to lash out when we wish we hadn't, make ill-advised business moves and do things that hurt others. This is a fact of life.

The most successful people are the ones that rebound from a setback. If you make a "mistake" or take part in a bad choice, just move on and do the next right thing. Try not to dwell on the past mistake, just accept it, move on and move forward. Do the next right thing.

The Worst Case Scenario - Defeating yourself before you begin

There is safety and security in failing. There is safety and security in thinking that you will fail. There is safety and security in not trying to improve your health and fitness levels. There is safety and security in talking about how you will fail and how you are not worthy of success, in how you do everything wrong and do nothing right.

RESULTS

excellent ☐

good ☐

satisfactory ☐

poor ☒

In my experience this type of self-talk is a cover up of your fears and takes the pressure off of taking action. I am going to go out on a limb and guess that you are achieving poor results in one or more areas of your life right now using this type of thought process and language. Unless you choose to change it you will continue to achieve the same type of result.

Talking about how hard something is, how bad you are at something, or will be at something or how badly you will fail and have failed in the past simply does not help you. Besides, aren't you failing with what you are doing now anyway?

Go ahead, give it a try. I am sure that you will impress yourself and breed some positive motivation. The way to overcome doubt is with action.

Reasons vs Excuses

Evaluate your self-talk and your discussions with others. Are you coming up with excuses as to why you fail or are you accepting responsibility for your action and moving forward?

A _Reason_ is out of your direct control. There is nothing you can do about a reason (genetics, injury, environmental and/or disaster). An _Excuse_ is directly under your control (Lack of movement, overeating, watching too much T.V., and not paying your bills on time).

List your "Go To" Excuses:

Habit Goals vs Outcome Goals

When we are tied to an outcome we often end up dissatisfied with our result. Most people I have encountered that are "attached" to the outcome are always dissatisfied with the pace of change and give up before reaching the goal itself.

When people are attached to improvement through better habits they will generally succeed. Change takes time. Give yourself the time and the patience it takes to succeed by focusing on what you are doing, not on what you are or are not getting.

An example of an Outcome Goal is - "I want to be a millionaire."
An example of a Habit Goal is -

- "I will wake up one hour earlier every day."
- "I will read Biographies of truly successful people."
- "I will surround myself with positive/intelligent and supportive people."
- "I will strive for excellence in all that I do and accept no shortcuts."
- "I will spend my money wisely and begin to save for my future."

Can you see how these Habit Goals will bring you closer to your Outcome Goal?

Justification and Judgments

For many of us, we become masters at justifying our behaviors and actions. We tend to blame outside forces or claim uncontrollable circumstances are responsible for our bad luck and poor results...

In reality, we are in control of much more than we think and when someone finally takes control of their circumstances and situation it is then, finally, that they realize how much control and power they were giving away.

You control who your friends are and how much interaction you have with them. You control your support system. You created it. If it is not a supportive one then you are responsible for changing that because no one else will do it for you.

Many of us also tend to accept harsh and unhelpful judgments from people. We will forego listening to our internal voice and may not act on what we know to be best for ourselves. Whether it is that we go out to dinner because we succumbed to peer pressure or have a dessert we really did not wish to consume nor had more alcohol when we felt we were finished already. Be your own person.

It is AMAZING what happens to excuses when you decide to make the EXCUSES go away.

Don't Let Perfect Get In The Way of Better

Minimizing carelessness and mindlessness is a realistic goal. Eliminating mistakes is impossible. Everyone makes mistakes. Some are larger than others and can be overcome easily with the proper mindset.

You will make mistakes and make decisions and choices that, in retrospect, you wish you hadn't. This is just part of life.

Take your time, accept your decision and own the results. When you are wrong, admit it and let go of THAT decision. Make the next decision and repeat.

Raise your Expectations.

If you want more for yourself, you must expect more of yourself.

Until now you have been satisfied (or at least not dissatisfied enough) with what you have and what/who you are. When you make the decision that you want more from yourself and your life it becomes time to change your expectations, your priorities and your actions. In order meet your new

expectations (desires), you must determine what knowledge base and skills you have now and determine which new skills and knowledge you need to be successful.

Raise the standards you have maintained and evolve toward being a better and different you.

You want more, now you must act and think differently in order to BE different.

Great Ideas Vanish.

When you have a brainstorm or a great idea enters your head it is generally recommended to stop what you are doing and make 60 seconds worth of notes, or even a quick outline.

How many times have you had a great idea to only be unable to recall it later? Act then return immediately to what you were doing.

Control what you can control.

Accept the facts and move on.

I have experienced many people that get upset over past events, experiences, and situations that have already occurred. Almost as if they choose to hold on to the frustration that the events caused at the time. I also experience people getting upset over things that have little to do with them and ultimately will not mean much in the near or distant future. If this is you AND you are an emotional eater, you may want to consider just how damaging this way of thinking is to your health fitness goals. This is not to suggest that you not feel empathy or not wish the best for yourself or anyone else. It is to suggest that you need to care for yourself the best that you can, and that you owe yourself that much. If external events are "controlling" your decision-making and it affects your food choices, energy level, and activity level, then I ask – What will change? Nothing happens physically if it does not happen mentally first.

Stress Reduction Kit

Directions:
1. Place kit on FIRM surface.
2. Follow directions in circle of kit.
3. Repeat step 2 as necessary, or until unconscious.
4. If unconscious, cease stress reduction activity.

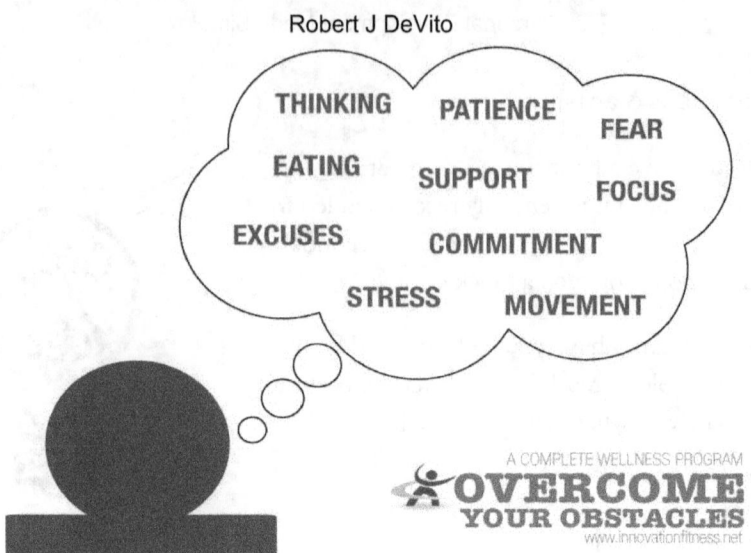

THINKING PATIENCE FEAR
EATING SUPPORT FOCUS
EXCUSES COMMITMENT
STRESS MOVEMENT

A COMPLETE WELLNESS PROGRAM
OVERCOME
YOUR OBSTACLES
www.innovationfitness.net

Fact vs. Feeling: Objective vs. Subjective

Feelings are not facts. They are feelings. Emotions are feelings and are completely separate from facts. Attempt to keep your feelings from becoming "your reality facts" in your life. Many individuals allow what they feel to become "fact" and dictate their actions.

Have you ever said, "I feel fat"? You may have overeaten by calories and volume for a meal or even a whole day and as a result, you FEEL bloated, full and fat. Factually, you may have eaten a few hundred extra calories and a few hundred milligrams extra of sodium, which is causing the physical feeling. If this caries over emotionally and alters your actions the following day, this is where the problem lies. I call this type of action "**consistent inconsistency**". This will result in a cycle of eating too much one-day, not eating enough the following day, then overeating again the next day…

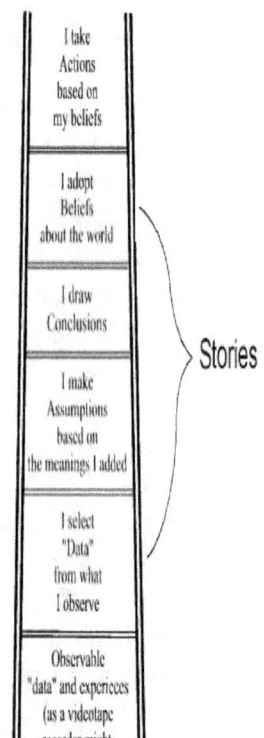

I take Actions based on my beliefs

I adopt Beliefs about the world

I draw Conclusions

I make Assumptions based on the meanings I added

I select "Data" from what I observe

Observable "data" and experiences (as a videotape recorder might capture it)

Stories

Feel your feelings but layer the logic on top of them to understand if what you're feeling is emotional or a reality. React accordingly. Over time, you will begin to see the facts THEN layer the emotions. This is where true productivity and a proactive lifestyle rule.

The "One-upsmanship" of Negativity

Let me guess. You were really busy and rushed today, people were inconsiderate and stupid and no one in your company is remotely close to being competent, never mind productive. Traffic was a nightmare, you are starving and you just do not have time to think about exercise, eating right nor doing anything for you because you are too busy doing for others. Yet, when you explain yourself to people and give them your "excuse list" they actually have the gall to have a bigger, longer list and it just so happens that you thought that you had a bad day but it actually pales in comparison to the even more negative person you are conversing with. Sound familiar?

Many of us live in an environment where if things are bad (and they usually are)

THIS IS YOUR **LIFE.**
DO WHAT YOU LOVE,
AND DO IT OFTEN.
IF YOU DON'T LIKE SOMETHING, CHANGE IT.
IF YOU DON'T LIKE YOUR JOB, QUIT.
IF YOU DON'T HAVE ENOUGH TIME, STOP WATCHING TV.
IF YOU ARE LOOKING FOR THE LOVE OF YOUR LIFE, STOP;
THEY WILL BE WAITING FOR YOU WHEN YOU
START DOING THINGS YOU LOVE.
STOP OVER ANALYZING, ALL EMOTIONS ARE BEAUTIFUL.
LIFE IS SIMPLE. EVERY LAST BITE. WHEN YOU EAT, APPRECIATE
OPEN YOUR MIND, ARMS, AND HEART TO NEW THINGS
AND PEOPLE, WE ARE UNITED IN OUR DIFFERENCES.
ASK THE NEXT PERSON YOU SEE WHAT THEIR PASSION IS,
AND SHARE YOUR INSPIRING DREAM WITH THEM.
TRAVEL OFTEN; GETTING LOST WILL HELP YOU FIND YOURSELF.
SOME OPPORTUNITIES ONLY COME ONCE, SEIZE THEM.
LIFE IS ABOUT THE PEOPLE YOU MEET, AND
THE THINGS YOU CREATE WITH THEM
SO GO OUT AND START CREATING.
LIFE IS LIVE YOUR DREAM,
SHORT. **AND WEAR** YOUR PASSION.

someone has it much worse than you ever could. The "one upsmanship" of negativity breeds, spreads, and kills any chance for you to be positive – unless you are mentally strong enough to find the positive aspect in every situation.

You will always be busy, overworked, tired, rushed, hurried, negative, worried, and anxious and surrounded by negativity until you choose not to be. Choose to see the positive side if things first and you will be happier and life will slow down.

Consider how your mood and environment affect your decision making.

First things First

Creating a daily plan of action is vital to success. I like to group my work by "Urgent/ Must do" and decrease the importance from there. It keeps me "on task". These tasks allow me to accomplish quite a bit of IMPORTANT and

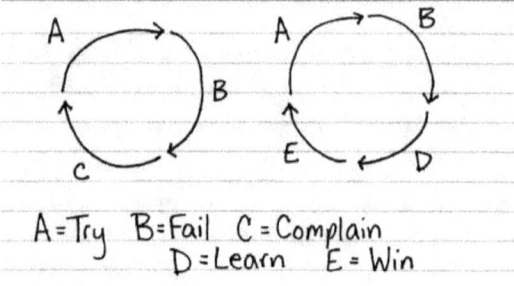

PRODUCTIVE work throughout the day. They are the habits that move my day and life forward.

One of the most useful things I have done is used the 4th column "Not Important" to list out all of my time wasters. It is estimated that people "waste" 4 hours per day.

Take the 15- minutes it requires daily to plan your success. It will save you untold amounts of time. One prominent figure estimates saving 1 hour 45 minutes daily.

Listing your time wasters can be a startling revelation to where all of your time goes. One of the biggest culprits I see is when people get distracted easily. Stops and starts rob you of momentum and creates difficulty for task completion.

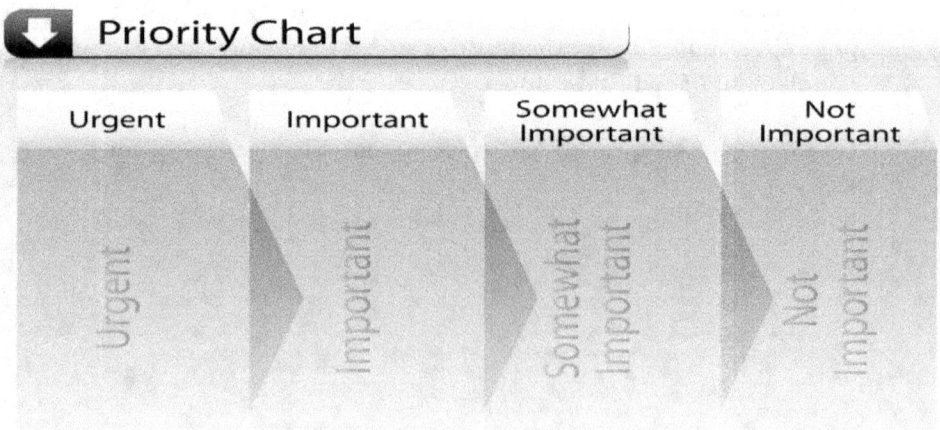

Consistent Application of Proven Principles

Take the information in this book, apply your integrity and hard work and make your life what you want it to be.

Get Going.

No more waiting. The time for change is now.

I would wish you luck, but luck has NOTHING to do with your success.

The #1 SECRET to success.

There is no secret and there is no magic formula for success.

Success takes effort, persistence, dedication, planning and solid strategies. That is the formula.

THE AUTHOR

Robert J DeVito is the President and Chief Motivational Officer for Innovation Fitness Solutions He has 20 years of experience in the fitness and personal development industries. Robert has helped 1000's of individuals reach their lifestyle goals by understanding their motivations, their bodies and making solid choices.
"Simple" features information on understanding how to relieve stress, break through weight loss barriers and overcome your life obstacles. It gives you the tools to apply these principles to your life now.

Where "Simple" truly shines IS in its simplicity. The chances are good that you have at least two "Self-Help" books that you bought with great intentions and never got past page 10... Surely the books are filled with great information, so it must be the overwhelming size and confusing layouts that prevent you from completing the reading. You will use "Simple" as a reference tool to help create your best life.

RDeVitoIFS   **www.Facebook.com/InnovationFitness**